A JOHN CATT PUBLICATION

— JAMIE THO

SLO..
TEACHING

ON FINDING CALM, CLARITY AND IMPACT IN THE CLASSROOM

C000149001

First Published 2018

by John Catt Educational Ltd,
12 Deben Mill Business Centre, Old Maltings Approach,
Melton, Woodbridge IP12 1BL

Tel: +44 (0) 1394 389850 Fax: +44 (0) 1394 386893
Email: enquiries@johncatt.com
Website: www.johncatt.com

ISBN: 978 1 911382 60 7

Set and designed by John Catt Educational Limited

CONTENTS

FOREWORD

Now is the time to pause, now is the time to reflect and now is the time consider the notion that fast is better than slow. And *Slow Teaching* provides an important counterpoint and a prompt for doing so. At a time when the speed of events, overwhelming visual stimuli, expectations of work being completed in the quickest possible time threaten to overwhelm us, we need a coherent explanation and rationale for stepping back, taking stock and refreshing our thinking. And this is what 'Slow Teaching' does.

It is a meditation on the importance of slow. It is timely in that it addresses some of the issues highlighted daily in staffrooms, on social media and indeed from the DfE's workload review. However, instead of locating the arguments at the strategic level, it provides a framework for personal reflection and action. It focuses on what each of us, as individuals, can do in order to slow down and paradoxically create better work.

Drawing on wide ranging research and ancient philosophy to back up his arguments, Jamie has translated his thesis on 'slow' into a meaningful commentary on the different aspects of our professional and personal lives. As such it will resonate with anyone involved in education. Furthermore, it will provide the insights, phrases and if needed, ammunition, when talking and debating with colleagues about what we are doing in our professional practice, and why. For too long we have taken the given, as given and now is the time to ask why, to strip back anything that is redundant and any process or practice which does not make a contribution to learning.

The book provides us with the prompts to ask: how much of what we do is really necessary, how much of it is 'just the way things have always been done' and what can we realistically abandon without compromising quality? *Slow Teaching* provides us with the tools to have robust conversations about what is really necessary and what can be shredded.

Jamie's thesis is grounded in his own experiences. This makes it a joy to read, as there is something very powerful about a serious book, drawn on reflections of experience and located in wider research. There will be sighs and exclamations from the reader as they recognise their own practice and similar contexts. This is what gives the book real power, because it is drawn from the well of experience, of overdoing things, of 'going the extra mile' at considerable personal and professional cost. Jamie isn't the only one who has overdone things and whose body has reclaimed its balance by enforced inactivity.

'Slow Teaching' covers a broad spectrum including talk, classroom practice, relationships, classroom design, planning, feedback, wellbeing and surprisingly 'sacred silence'. I am delighted to see silence covered as a topic: the power of silence, of thinking time, of concentration, of deep thought, to hold a response, to just wait to see what emerges, without the need for constant chatter: all these aspects of silence are neglected in our discussions about high quality provision. So, it is particularly welcome to see this opened up in the book and I am sure it will stimulate a great deal of debate.

Slow Teaching also tackles some of the sector's own self-imposed stresses such as the curse of perfectionism, and ridiculous mantra such as 'A good teacher is like a candle – it consumes itself to light the way for others' (Theobald, 2017). It is healthy to open up this debate and we need more professionals stripping away at the myth of self-imposed martyrdom.

When the notion of 'slow' is unpacked and explained, it becomes clear that it has implications for every aspect of professional practice: and no more so that in the classroom. And what will result from this attention to 'slow', when we reconsider the essentials is focused, calmer and ultimately better learning. And that, after all, is the holy grail.

As with all the great insights in life, simplicity is easier said than done. However, in taking the elements of professional practice and considering them through the slow lens, these are made concrete and really helpful. The questions for self-reflection at the end of each chapter are astute and have the power to keep us on track. They would serve as useful additions to departmental and leadership meetings. Because ultimately, the pursuit of 'slow' is about doing things for the right reasons.

Slow Teaching is an important book, which will help all of us to pause, take a deep breathe and take stock. I wholeheartedly recommend educators to read it. Slowly.

Mary Myatt, January 2018

For Fiona.

There is no one I admire more; thank you for everything.

PART I: SILENT SLOW

CHAPTER 1: THE SLOW TEACHING PHILOSOPHY

There is more to life than increasing its speed.
Mahatma Gandhi

You have taken the first step: hesitantly opening the pages of this book. There may be elements of doubt in your mind as you recall the repertoire of more fashionable and effective teaching behaviours, a speed-induced cocktail with the ingredients of pace, energy and engagement.

You pause, questioning the connotations of the adjective 'slow' in the all-consuming, rapid-paced world of education.

A first memory arises of that exhausted feeling on a Friday evening after a week on the relentless conveyer belt of school life. A second memory recalls those huge piles of workbooks, each strewn with red pen as your aching hand scribbles yet another repetitive comment. A third is more emotional: how regularly you feel utterly overwhelmed by the endless demands on your time.

You then remember the hordes of eager, inspired faces that joined you on that nerve-wracking, exciting first day of teacher training. Those motivated and passionate individuals, a significant number of whom now no longer teach. A flicker of recognition (or, dare I say, hope) briefly overcomes you as you reflect again on the title: *Slow Teaching*.

My work begins.

This book has an agenda. I will be very clear from the beginning. It will seek to highlight the value of slowing down in almost everything we do in education. It will challenge popular whirlwind teaching priorities: 'outstanding' single teaching episodes; obsessional data collection; endless marking; single lesson performance management; sporadic behaviour management systems and the priority on engagement over learning.

Instead, *Slow Teaching* will highlight the value of the considered, reflective and mindful teacher, whose ability to slow down both inside and outside of the classroom energises them, and results in improved progress for the students in their care. It will explore teaching for real impact; teaching that focuses on retaining knowledge and that enables a lifelong love of learning. We will see how this requires patient development over time, with real attention to detail.

It will recognise that learning is messy and anything but linear, arguing that measured teaching for retention and memory is a skill that is still not given enough priority in our schools. Feedback strategies that move students forward in their learning and maximise the use of teachers' precious time will be explored, alongside assessments that are carefully considered and will equip teachers with the tools to plan for the success of all their students. The streamlined focus will be on what will have the most influence in moving learning forward, not on fulfilling an Ofsted agenda or a data imperative.

We will pause to reflect on the experience of education for young people, whose lives are overwhelmed by the relentless world of social media and technology addictions. *Slow Teaching* will argue that our classrooms should be sanctuaries of routine, patience and calm that teach vital 'slow' skills: listening, concentration and most importantly the capacity to reflect and think about learning. It will explore how this will allow us to build better relationships and appreciate the daily joys and nuances of teaching.

Continuing to improve this craft will also be a priority in the pages of this book: prioritising the deliberate, reflective and research-based practice that will allow you to continue to grow and become an expert in your field. In short, this book aims to help you to rediscover your passion for the wonderful world of teaching. It will also examine school management and reflect on how the slow leadership style – with its focus on attention to detail – can provide the framework to empower students and give them the very best opportunities in life.

This book arrives at a junction in education at which the use of 'crisis' is becoming more ubiquitous. Hardly a day goes by without a screaming headline: 'crisis' in teacher retention, 'crisis' in teachers sprinting to leave the profession, 'crisis' in confidence in school leadership, and 'crisis' in attracting teachers to work in more challenging environments. Political interference has arguably resulted in more reactive policies that fail to provide long-term solutions. There is a clear void, a lack of proactive and considered reflection in education, hindering our ability to move the profession forward – inch by inch, painstakingly slow, step by step.

We will consider what the reality of wellbeing really means in a school environment, evaluating how best we can develop a better understanding and relationship with stress. Sharing practical and sustainable strategies to equip teachers with the ability to enjoy a long, positive and healthy career in teaching will be one of the residing aims of *Slow Teaching*.

This book is also the product of a personal odyssey of embracing a slower and more reflective professional life. The beginning of my own teaching career was particularly frenzied, with an early promotion to assistant headteacher in a large comprehensive school in central London. For years I literally ran three miles into school, dashed around manically for long hours on autopilot, then ran home laden with stacks of books to keep me company into the late evening.

I was utterly invincible: thriving on little sleep and the adrenaline of pace. Signs of exhaustion and the build-up of all-encompassing stress were arrogantly rejected. I coped by moving with more and more urgency; a self-defeating and relentless life of pace. Mistakes in my professional and private life gradually built up and I became more fractured and more irritable. Any ability to think strategically or consider how best to manage my time was lost in the wildfire of cortisone and adrenaline that comes with a life fuelled by stress.

I ignored the clear signals, driving myself further and further into the ground. It culminated in illness, professional burnout and an almost complete refutation of the teaching profession. I was close to joining the legions of teachers whose early experience in education left them demoralised and defeated by a relentless profession.

The transition to becoming a more tranquil individual has been one of tears, sweat and anxiety. The explosion of mindfulness literature and the growing cultural shift towards slowing down has been a guiding light in the darkness. Stumbling across texts such as *In Praise of Slow* by Carl Honore and *The Things You Can See Only When You Slow Down* by Haemin Sunim have helped me in developing a new philosophy that appreciates the calm, the contemplative and the merits of slowing down. This journey has included reflection on how the individuals who professed to slow tendencies – including Nelson Mandela, Mahatma Gandhi and the Stoic philosophers – achieved such success through a deliberate rejection of speed. As the chapters that follow demonstrate, it has also led me to invest much more time in reflecting on, and learning from, the writings of others on education.

There is no idealism or romanticism in *Slow Teaching*: teaching will always be a demanding profession and young people are challenging customers who, inevitably, are the complete contrast of slow. The criteria that opened this introduction will continue to be essential in securing their progress. Yet, pace can also be overrated: it needs to be coupled with essential slow skills, forgotten aspects of teaching and learning that could ultimately prove transformative in securing positive futures for students.

It is time to control the mad theology of speed that is damaging the teaching profession; to press pause and reflect on an educational system that is being stretched to its limits. It is time to streamline teaching to focus on what can make a difference for young people, something that can only be achieved if we deliberately slow down and focus on what matters. Let the journey slowly begin...

CHAPTER 2: THE MINIMALISTIC CLASSROOM

Simplicity is the ultimate sophistication.
Leonardo da Vinci

It is an image familiar in schools throughout the country: the red-faced, exhausted and agitated teacher, surrounded by streams of student books, with paper strewn haphazardly around their desk. The walls are covered in faded, yellowing posters, with the obligatory rules of the classroom dog-eared and (tragically) ignored. The chairs and tables embrace this atmosphere: they are misaligned, disjointed and decorated with chewing gum. Into this environment stumbles the next class...

We are too busy and too rushed by more pressing priorities to consider one of the most important projections of our psychological state in the school environment: our classrooms. What would be the impact of turning them into an oasis of calm and organisation? Would pausing to prioritise the appearance and organisation of our classrooms generate better relationships and learning?

Instant Judgements
It might appear questionable to reflect on Malcolm Gladwell's *Blink* in a book that is promoting a more measured and thoughtful professional approach. Gladwell's text is about our instant judgements and the decisions that we make without real thought; the complete contrast of slow thinking. It explores our capacity to make lasting judgements, based entirely on first impressions. In *Blink*, Gladwell (2007) notes how the psychologist Nalini Ambady provided students with a clip of a teacher, and asked for their ratings of the teacher's effectiveness:

> A person watching a silent two-second video tape of a teacher he or she has never met, will reach conclusions about how good that teacher is that are very similar to those of a student who has sat in the teacher's class for an entire semester. That's the power of our adaptive unconscious.

It is a revealing insight into just how quickly students make decisions about teachers, judgments that are often fixed and difficult to influence. In the privacy of these pages we can also, perhaps, secretly admit to the power of our own adult 'adaptive unconscious'; our innate biases. Instant judgements, decisions and actions are an essential component of our everyday experience. Although we may not like to admit it, within minutes of entering the home of a new acquaintance we begin to form impressions about them. How often have these intuitions proved lasting and influential in how we respond to people?

As teachers, and as victims of these quick judgements, there is a more important question for us to consider: what can we do to ensure a more positive instant impression that will have lasting impact?

The Influence of the Classroom

The classroom is a teacher's unconscious arena – it projects powerful subliminal messages to those who enter. Its makeup will, in part, influence how students respond to our teaching and their motivation in our subjects. There is nothing more hypocritical than berating a student for sloppy presentation, or a lack of attention to detail, when our own classroom does not provide a visible example of the level of care we desire. Students are aware of this; they are attuned to the clarity and integrity of the messages we deliver.

Our classroom environment is also more important than we think in influencing levels of concentration and focus. There is evidence to suggest that a cluttered environment filled with visual chaos directly impacts on students' ability to process information. This was one of the conclusions reached by Fisher *et al* in the 2014 experiment 'Visual environment, attention allocation, and learning in young children: when too much of a good thing may be bad'. After conducting lessons with younger children in both a decorated classroom and a sparse classroom, they discovered that students were less likely to remain focused in a highly decorated classroom and, additionally, they achieved lower test scores. It is perhaps obvious: visual stimulation directly influences and impacts on how well students are concentrating on their learning. A lack of focus on presenting a calm environment may well be hindering the ability of the students in our classrooms to think and to retain information.

The classroom is also the place where both teachers and students spend significant portions of their day and, at times, it can feel like inordinately more time than in our own homes. It therefore requires deliberate and careful engineering to ensure that we can function at our best. Importantly, by doing this we also take the first step towards positively influencing how we feel about our profession.

Richard H. Thaler and Cass R. Sunstein's (2010) *Nudge* is the fundamental basis for much of the new thinking on psychology and behavioural economics. It is a fascinating read when reflecting on the impact of creating an environment that is fit for purpose. The authors note that 'small and apparently insignificant details can have major impacts on people's behaviour'. The authors also highlight the impact that rearranging school cafeterias has in promoting healthier nutritional choices by students, stating that 'school children, like adults, can be greatly influenced by small changes in the context'.

With this in mind, what small changes can we make to our classroom environment? Perhaps a useful starting point would be to tackle the clutter.

Decluttering

One of the issues in the modern classroom is the ubiquity of 'stuff' that dominates every spare inch of the room. There are resources, workbooks and equipment all desperately vying for the limited space available. There can also be the temptation to couple this with ornate visual displays, with every space on the walls covered in painstakingly created visual stimulation. When combined this can leave teachers struggling to access the clear thinking that is vital for effective teaching. It is impossible to function efficiently when our brains are overwhelmed and cluttered – and this is especially true of our working environment.

At the start of my teaching career I was a chief hoarder: all paper resources and books were jammed into overflowing cupboards and shelves. I couldn't bring myself to get rid of anything, holding on to the misguided belief that it would come in handy at some point (if I could find it!) I also convinced myself that I did not have time to develop any real organisation of the classroom: the workbooks and marking won every argument to do with time management. This served only to feed and increase the ferocity of the newly qualified teacher (NQT) anxiety monster. I spent mornings frantically pulling out pieces of paper, desperately hunting for another misplaced student book, working my way up towards panic even before any students entered the room. Never did I ask myself the questions that only the space of experience and reflection can encourage: how much of what I was hoarding was necessary? How much of it directly impacts on the learning of young people in the classroom?

Minimalism

Minimalism is a movement growing in popularity, driven by a modern culture that is obsessive about the collecting and hoarding of 'stuff'. It argues instead for a decluttering of our lives to facilitate a calmer and more organised method of living and working. The principles are based on prioritisation and the frequent clearing out of all that is unnecessary: an essential practice in avoiding the collection of wheelbarrows' worth of extra material in the classroom.

S.J. Scott and Barrie Davenport (2012) highlight that 'all this extraneous stuff not only sucks our time and productivity, but also produces reactive, anxious and negative thoughts'. This triplet of emotions is certainly not what we want in our classrooms, particularly when seeking to balance the diverse moods that thirty boisterous students can bring into our rooms. So, how can we embrace this first step to a more serene, considered life and establish a new minimalist approach to our classroom environment?

Commit to a Minimalist Review

Familiarisation breeds a lack of perspective. We may believe that our classrooms are indeed streamlined and organised but, as we shall see in the pages of this book, overconfidence and a lack of perspective is symptomatic of rushed thinking. Take time to slow down and ask the honest question: are we secret teacher magpies? Take fifteen minutes to look at your classroom from a new point of view. Sit in one of the students' seats and examine the environment from their perspective. Reflect objectively on the following questions: what image am I projecting? How much of the environment is helpful in enabling students to learn and concentrate? Consider the words of Shaa Wasmund (2016):

> Think of a well-run restaurant kitchen; not only is the food delicious, cooked on time and beautifully presented, behind the scenes everything is clean, ordered and uncluttered so that the chefs can focus on the task at hand. From simplicity comes focus and purpose.

Slowly walk around and inspect all those dusty corners and drawers in the room. What has been used recently? Question the function of everything. How essential are the various paper documents that are surreptitiously hiding? Could they be transposed into electronic versions?

Be Ruthless

We all know the wonderful lightness of spirit that we experience when we have undertaken a 'spring clean' of our homes. Keep this image of serenity in mind when you undergo the first intimidating minimalist review of your classroom. This is best undertaken just before the start of a new term or school year, another step towards facilitating the notion of a new start or new beginning.

Joshua Fields Millburn and Ryan Nicodemus (2012) state to begin this process 'with the easy things: the superfluous clothes jammed in the closet, the junk drawers teeming with junk, the unused kitchenware taking up space just in case'. While the odds of having lots of clothes in your classroom are low (I hope!), paper and equipment are the most likely to be the guilty targets. You may find yourself seeking to justify every element of your room: don't listen to the doubting, hording-infested mindset. That poster that seems to communicate important behavioural values in the room has probably not been looked at for some time; it is about the clarity and consistency of your messaging in the room, not a poster.

This step is easiest with equipment. You may be genuinely surprised by the range of things in the classroom that don't work or are broken. Get rid of anything that is surplus to requirements. Now, move towards the paper; here is where your new friend, the scanner, will be hugely enabling. If in doubt, go electronic – copy and save to that wonderful decluttering device, the trusty memory stick or shared drive (although, remember the memory stick itself is ripe for decluttering and may need a minimalist review!)

If you are fortunate enough to have a desk then this is perhaps the most important of the minimalist tools. There is a clear rationale for keeping only what is essential on the teacher desk: the teacher planner, the pen, the computer. Experts argue to limit personal items to three or less, otherwise this can lead to distraction. As Tony Crabbe (2015) notes, 'Your brain is possibly the most complex object in the universe; it's amazing, but it's not designed for the level of demand, distraction and stimulation you are throwing at it'. Applying a streamlined approach to the desk will breed clarity of thinking, a lucidity that will then filter into other aspects of your work.

Sustain the Minimalism

This is the challenging part. We may glow with joy as we look around our new sparse classroom walls and shelves and even allow ourselves some internal massaging: 'My word. I am organised.' Yet, sustaining this new minimalist habit is challenging.

For a long time I lapsed back into bad habits (and I still do). In the day-to-day rush of school life it becomes easy to horde, to shove things back into the nearest cave rather than look for proactive solutions. The solution lies in *10-Minute Declutter: The Stress-Free Habit for Simplifying Your Home* (2015) by S.J. Scott and Barrie Davenport. The principle is simple and refreshing: commit to ten minutes of decluttering every day. While every minute is indeed precious in our daily work, the ten-minute investment in this habit will have a positive impact. Leaving our classrooms at the end of the day in a position of organisation and structure will leave you feeling reassured and result in you starting the next day with clarity. The alternative is that you might mark one or two more books; the book can wait but the lucidity of your thinking and feelings of control cannot.

Embracing the minimalist lifestyle should also make you reflect carefully about your relationship one of the time devils on our shoulder: the photocopier. How much time is invested in making endless paper copies in the daily life of a teacher? Is it really essential in moving learning forward? Could it be replaced with something that will take less time to prepare and take up less space in the classroom? It will also seep into your relationships with other elements that we will explore later: emails, photocopying, planning and even your teaching itself. Simplicity and clarity will begin to become your automatic behaviours.

Share the Purpose

Our classrooms are visited by a diverse cast of students during the course of the week. Sharing this new refined classroom project, trying to encourage the sense of ownership and collective minimalism attitude will help to sustain the habit. Be possessive and fussy about it: while most will embrace the challenge there will always be the minority who need frequent repetition and reminders. I have learned from watching teachers who are skilled classroom organisers, who speak about their classrooms as sanctuaries of organisation and clarity and demand that their students return this with the upmost of respect. They fixate on the order of chairs and tables, sweating the small stuff so that students embrace the whole. Importantly, these teachers walk the walk, modelling values and presentation. As an observer in the classroom it is fascinating to watch how this control over environment is often hugely empowering in improving direction and learning in lessons.

Organisation

This new minimalist classroom will not function in isolation. It requires structure to make sure the room radiates with organisation. Daniel J. Levitin's book *The Organized Mind* (2015) argues that even if we are a 'creative' individual we can still implement systems to sustain organisation and protect our psychological comfort: thus, 'the more carefully constructed your categories, the more organized is your environment and, in turn, your mind.' Slowing down to manage the organisation of the classroom is an essential step, allowing us to reflect on the detail and structures in place. It will, in turn, make us more efficient and paradoxically quicker in our environments.

Embrace the Labels

Cultivating a labelling obsession is a sure-fire way to assist in creating an organised environment, particularly if everything is clearly identified. Marking the labels of different teaching groups and marking the labels of drawers in which equipment is stored will ensure that you have a clear understanding of everything in your room. The days of manic hair pulling as you search for that vital document will be over. Labelling is also a powerful tool for students: they know exactly where to find everything they need to assist in their learning.

Storage boxes can also become an important ally. Box everything to ensure that space is maximised, including the pesky collections of student books. Doing this means that it will be easy to find student books in future, as they are labelled and stored in a box in a designated area of the classroom. Sorted.

Individualise

Develop your own systems that enable a confidence and clarity about how you maintain organisation in your classroom. Instead of becoming a resources magpie, become an organisation magpie. As Levitin (2015) notes, 'It is important to harmonize your organisational style and systems with your personality'.

Excellence

While embodying an organised, streamlined and focused environment is vital in creating a calm classroom culture, there is one other element that we would ideally want our classrooms to reflect: excellence in our subjects. There is no doubt that our classrooms are influential in communicating the passion we have for our subject and the nature of standards expected in the room. A classroom that displays quality pieces of work is subconsciously raising the standards for those students who aspire to achieve them.

The opposite is also true. A piece of work that is displayed without these values may well communicate low expectations. This may well be my pet hate as an English teacher: student work that is proudly displayed but full of uncorrected literacy errors communicates all of the wrong signals about learning in the classroom.

In order to do this, we need to become what Ron Berger (2003) defines as 'a historian of excellence':

> One of my jobs as a teacher, I feel, is to be an historian of excellence, an archiver of excellence. Wherever I am, in my school or in other schools throughout the country, I am on the lookout for models of beautiful

work, powerful work, important work. These examples set the standards for what I am my students aspire to achieve in school.

Classroom displays can quickly merge into wallpaper, functioning merely as a backdrop. The hours of painstaking effort put in to create these displays will have an immediate 'gasp' effect but, sadly for our sleep deprived minds they will then be quickly forgotten. Becoming an 'archiver of excellence' will have a greater impact on inspiring students' to recognise what they are capable of achieving.

An English teacher I had the pleasure of working with had a 'Wall of Wonder' in their classroom which documented excellent pieces of student work. They would spend twenty minutes every fortnight adding to this space and changing the work that was displayed. (The psychological impact of this is significant: students are delighted when they receive the prestige of having their work documented.) The teacher would analyse the work with the class, explaining why it had reached the dizzying heights of the 'Wall of Wonder'.

A revolving cycle of effective student work can assist in sustaining cultures of excellence. It is also powerful in that it reminds us to demand more from students frequently, and creates a culture where students strive to meet the 'Wall of Wonder' standards.

Passionate Classrooms

A classroom that speaks nothing of the value and beauty of its subject is already missing vital opportunities to motivate students. On their travels across the school day, young people are remarkably sentient: they will absorb and reflect on the classroom environments that motivate them. We also want them to slow down, and recognise that they need to adapt to, and embrace, the thinking of the new subject they have arrived in.

In turn, we too need to pause and consider how much of the passion for our subject is visible in our classrooms. Consider how odd our home environment would be if it did not provide an insight into our personalities, our loved ones and our hobbies. The same applies to the classroom.

For me, it is very subtle: it is about making books ubiquitous in the classroom and communicating a passion and love of literature. There is a (methodically organised, obviously) library section in my classroom that highlights what myself and my students are reading. This selection of literature revolves and provides suggestions for students to consider reading. Thinking about the most streamlined and time-efficient ways to illuminate the enthusiasm we have for our subjects is one of the joys of the teaching profession.

Now that our physical environment has embraced a measured clarity that radiates with passion, sparse charm and organisation, we can turn our attention to the business of learning within our classrooms. We are not yet ready to welcome in our eager youngsters; instead, we need to reflect carefully on the best way we can plan for their long-term success.

Slow Questions

1. Is your classroom in need of a minimalist review?

2. What immediate changes could you make to ensure the clarity and organisation of your environment?

3. What would the impact of ten minutes of decluttering a day have on your psychological state?

4. What new organisational structures could you implement?

5. Does your classroom model student excellence?

6. Is the passion you have for your subject clear in your classroom?

CHAPTER 3: STREAMLINED PLANNING AND TEACHING

In this age, which believes there is a short cut to everything, the greatest lesson to be learned is that the most difficult way is, in the long run, the easiest.
Henry Miller

We are all familiar with the basic plot of Aesop's fable 'The Tortoise and The Hare'. It revolves around two contrasting figures: the speedy Hare and the slow Tortoise. The hare isn't the most modest of chaps; he frequently mocks the ponderous and plodding nature of the tortoise. Fed up with this ridicule, the plucky tortoise challenges the hare to a race. Having taken what he believes to be a clear lead, the hare decides to have a short slumber. Shock horror! – upon waking he finds that the tortoise has ambled his way into the lead and to eventual victory.

'The Tortoise and The Hare' in the Classroom
Allow me an extended analogy (more of the learning power of that later). This fable is a perfect representation of the contrast between teachers in a school environment. Mr Hare is the charismatic 'outstanding' lesson deliverer: his individual lessons sparkle with flair, dynamism and engagement. Students talk highly of him: 'Every lesson is so fun and interesting!' or 'We are never bored!' They dash for his lessons, waiting eagerly for whatever 'learning journey' will be tightly and energetically compressed into an hour. Mr Hare puts hours into manufacturing detailed PowerPoint slides that are full of stimulating images; he photocopies endless resources, and he has a particular penchant for group work tasks that are spectacularly well organised. There is an almost manic energy to Mr Hare; he moves all day with irresistible speed.

Mr Tortoise is a more self-deprecating classroom figure. His individual lessons are more refined, with his painstaking long-term plans providing the insight he needs to generate the individual experiences for his students. He has an almost-mythical knowledge of his subject; the product of intense investment in developing mastery of subject content. He rejected the default mode of PowerPoint slides some time ago, preferring to focus his students' full attention on the purpose of learning. His students may speak about him in a slightly less effusive manner, but what they do say is telling: 'We know what we need to do to improve.' 'He explains things for us so clearly.' 'He knows his subject inside out.' There is a serenity to Mr Tortoise's professional demeanour; he appears to glide through the day, omitting an aura of wisdom and experience.

In the examination race at the end of the year, senior management are bewildered and confused. Mr Tortoise's group performed much better, despite Mr Hare's 'outstanding' performance management lesson observation. Keen to learn from this experience, they set themselves a challenge: it is time to deconstruct, learn and share the practice of Mr Tortoise...

Learning Over Time

This is clearly an exaggerated stereotype, but it is an all too familiar distinction in modern day education. We should not, of course, completely reject the importance of an 'outstanding' individual lesson experience or, indeed, the power of some of Mr Hare's work in the classroom. Individual lessons of dynamism have much to offer. They remind students of the exciting potential of our subjects and learning in general, and can spark initial interest in a topic, which can result in immediate learning gains.

There is, however, a much more important conversation that needs to take priority: how to teach effectively over time. Teaching, and indeed learning, is not a series of isolated lesson-by-lesson experiences; it requires careful thinking and design.

In my first few years of teaching, I completely embraced Mr Hare's philosophy. I spent a disproportionate amount of time scrupulously studying how to achieve the holy grail of being awarded an Ofsted 'outstanding' lesson. For those precious observed moments, I would spend hours planning lessons of Oscar award winner potential, coupled with resources that were painstakingly constructed and differentiated for every child. My excellent mentor would (sometimes) say some lovely things, then pose the question: so what is the next step?

Cue awkward pause. Next step?

I had absolutely no idea how to plan for learning over time; how to look at sustaining learning; how to build on skills incrementally. Nobody had talked about that during my training. Instead they threw around 'engagement', 'collaboration', and 'learning styles' like confetti. I certainly don't recall hearing the word 'memory' at any point. In those early days, I would eagerly rush to see the magic pay off in students' assessments and then slump dejectedly into a corner: why wasn't any of the learning sticking?

I was a walking metaphor for what was wrong with the lesson-by-lesson approach. It left me utterly exhausted at the end of the working week, having lived on my nerves, without any clear sense of direction. The process of moving away from this – to reflect more on incremental learning over time – requires careful consideration of the best ways that students can learn. It is an investment that will pay off, as it provides us, in the words of Henry Ford (1928), with 'the calmness that the long view of life gives us'.

What influences the tendency to resort to a tunnel vision in respect of teacher planning? What results in sporadic lessons and weeks that lack coherence and a long term vision? Partly, it is circumstances ostensibly outside of our control: external pressure.

Performativity

Schools demand results; the government demands results, our pay is now often dictated by the results we can squeeze out of examination cohorts. This can mean that the 'fast fix' that will facilitate this 'success' is often used, and to invest time thinking about the long-term picture appears ludicrous. How many times have we heard the following: 'that is not a priority at this time of year'? This focus on results and achieving target grades leads to an approach that invests significantly more time in the upper echelons of the school environment, which can, at times, result in younger year groups not being given the attention they need.

The short-term implications of target grades also contribute to this myopic thinking, with 'what the spreadsheet says' reducing our capacity to think carefully about the future. As practitioners, we work relentlessly to secure the students their targets for that year, often missing opportunities to prepare them for further school (or indeed, life) experience.

When the inevitable panic hits, energy and time is thrown to the Grandfather of all quick fixes: intervention. Despite the limited research into its efficacy, intervention feels more immediate and secure as a method of achieving results. Yet, as we shall see, this seductive whisper of success often results in mindless doing, rather than thinking: feeding the hamster on the wheel that must keep spinning.

Time Constraints

Time is the devil on the shoulders of busy teachers. Its menacing tones follow us throughout the day, frequently urging us to move faster and faster, eating into any reflection we may have on the big picture and hindering our ability to think about long-term success. Conventionally, schools may benevolently allow us some 'strategic' thinking time at the end of the summer term, when exhaustion and apathy has begun to seep into the minds of even the most passionate of lesson planners. Before this point there is too much to do: books to mark, data to collect, individual lessons to 'sort'.

Inevitably, this results in planning that happens either late at night or early in the morning. Even the most conscientious of teachers take shortcuts in this mode of working, and without a sustainable and long-term vision, planning for retention and quality is often lost.

Yet, as we shall see, even as the factors outside of our immediate control roar their belligerent heads off: remember, it doesn't have to be this way. Our reactions to these external forces are completely within our control, and how we decide to maximise our time as teachers is the debate we need to have.

The Fast Brain

In gaining a better ability to plan for the long-term success of students, we need to first examine the tool that is so essential to our understanding of self and others: the human mind. Why is it that I was so focused on planning for day-by-day learning when I started teaching?

Well, first of all is the obvious point, as Henry Ford again highlights: 'Thinking is the hardest task there is, which is probably the reason why so few engage in it' (Ford: 1929) The modern world moves rapidly, resulting in us searching for quick fix solutions and languishing in tunnel vision thinking. Ultimately, this means that we are not as trained in the skills of strategic thinking as we perhaps should be. We are all tempted by the seductive call of the short-term: this is why the notification alert on mobile phones or the arrival of an email instantly distracts us from everything else. The effort and concentration that strategic planning requires is a much more challenging process. Combined with this are a series of biases that have a profound influence over how we think.

The Einstellung Effect

We are all, naturally, species of habit. We are predisposed to using tried-and-trusted strategies to solve problems – even when a better, simpler, more efficient strategy might exist. Our mechanisms of planning might well be fixed and could be defined by how we have approached this throughout our teaching careers. My frazzled mind could only function in this regimented lesson-by-lesson way of thinking: it was my default mode. I had never been guided or coached on how to look at building learning gradually over time.

Status Quo Bias

This, in part, explains our preference for wanting things to stay as they are, by doggedly sticking with decisions. The preference for inertia is often without any regard for the quality of the final output. We can often find ourselves psychologically and regimentally lodged in a status quo, a situation that can impact our ability to function successfully as practitioners in the classroom. How common are phrases like 'but we have always done it this way' in our staffrooms?

The Legacy Problem

The investment of time in a solution can result in people stubbornly standing with and defending it, regardless of how effective it is and without considering things from a different perspective. We often build up a number of lessons and resources for teaching topics, then regimentally plough on using them. Given the emotional investment in this process, it can be difficult to justify spending more time on a revamp.

The consequence of these troublesome biases is often a lack of dispassionate rationality; an inability to detach ourselves from our judgements and decision-making. Yet, as Daniel Kahneman (2015) notes, 'adding status quo bias, legacy problem and the Einstellung effect to everyday vocabulary can make it easier.' Becoming more aware of the way our minds can function will allow us to break away from thinking that may negatively influence our sense of direction for both young people and ourselves. We first need to reflect on the obvious question: what is it we are planning for?

The Planning Purpose

In *Secondary Assessment and Curriculum* (2016), Summer Turner provides a summary of 'Principled Curriculum Design' (originally compiled by Dylan Wiliam):

1. The 'intended' curriculum – the curriculum as prescribed by National Curriculum or equivalent: the specified topics, ideas, content that pupils should learn.

2. The 'implemented' curriculum the 'texts books, schemes of work, lesson plans'.

3. The 'enacted' curriculum – how this is translated into learning within the classroom, between the teacher and the pupil.

Turner's book provides an excellent overview of how to reflect on the intended curriculum. Now, we shall explore the individual teacher's sense of ownership over the 'enacted' curriculum. What can we, as classroom teachers, do to enable student success?

The Yearly Overview

A plan for the year is the first step. Very simply, this involves making decisions about what the year group will be studying through the course of the academic year. While this is often a collaborative process, or dictated by departmental decisions, it is vital as the classroom teacher that we have a comprehensive understanding of this. By doing so, we begin to break down and identify the overarching ideas that we want our students to have grasped by the time they finish the academic year.

Without taking time to carry out this planning, the academic year for the individual teacher becomes a process of mindless teaching; teaching merely to cover content and the curriculum, without any engagement with purpose and teaching over time.

It is also vital at this stage to ensure that the assessment for each unit of work is decided upon and shared with teachers. Knowing exactly what students are working towards enables teaching to be tailored for this particular focus, providing clarity and purpose for all involved.

The dialogue we have in department or collegiate teams about what we want each year group to achieve as they progress through school is another core element of our strategic planning. Generating skills and functional knowledge that they will have acquired at the end of each academic year will enable a continual upward trajectory of academic achievement. Importantly, it will also mean that teachers are aware of students' prior learning as they progress in our subjects, allowing us to build on these skills in each consecutive year.

The next priority is to break the yearly plan into the half-term units. Careful reflection is needed here about how the lessons will be connected, so as to assist in enabling student mastery of skills and content. Doug Lemov (2010) summarises the importance of this approach:

Unit planning means methodically asking how one day's lesson builds off the previous days, how it prepares for the next days, and how these all fit into a larger sequence of objectives that lead to mastery.

There are two important elements to facilitating this clear direction. Firstly, it is about ensuring our own deep understanding of subject content; then, secondly, distilling this knowledge down to provide the essential priorities for our students to learn.

Confident Content Knowledge

A deceptively simple, yet important question: how can we plan for a unit of work unless we have a detailed understanding of the content itself? Robert Coe *et al* (2014) conducted a comprehensive study of research which highlighted that pedagogical content knowledge had the most impact on student attainment:

> The most effective teachers have deep knowledge of the subjects they teach, and when teachers' knowledge falls below a certain level it is a significant impediment to students' learning. As well as a strong understanding of the material being taught, teachers must also understand the ways students think about the content, be able to evaluate the thinking behind students' own methods, and identify students' common misconceptions.

Often, we will dive headfirst into planning and teaching a topic without having invested the measured thinking that should go into reflecting on the content knowledge. Our glittering degrees and string of qualifications may give us the mistaken confidence that we can approach our subjects blindfolded. This overconfidence may result in missing vital learning opportunities for our students.

When we are insecure about our subject knowledge, our anxiety levels are elevated; often, subconsciously, we are waiting to be caught out. The greater the sense of control we have over the content we teach students, the more confident we are and the more effective our teaching is. Being confident in our content knowledge helps us to seem authentic; it gives us the calm clarity and purposefulness that implies we know exactly where students are going and how to get them there. Combined with this is the sense of mastery over exam specifications and model answers, which further equips us with the ownership required to teach effectively over time.

Acquiring a deep level of content knowledge requires a large investment of time and for us to step off the teacher carousel of activity. The importance

31

of thinking through which misconceptions students might have is a vital process, allowing us to see the learning through their eyes. This empathetic skill will not only make us more compassionate teachers, but will mean that we can plan better to address their needs going forward. Once we have our own understanding completely secure, we then seek to simplify the core elements of the unit for our students.

The Knowledge Organisers

Joe Kirby, Deputy Headteacher at Michaela School in London, calls these 'the most powerful tool in the arsenal of the curriculum designer' (Birbalsingh, 2016). The premise of the knowledge organiser is very simple: it collects all the vital information that students need to know for the unit of work together on a single page. This may include important information and concepts, vital vocabulary linked to the topic and key explanations of terms.

There is real discipline in the process of making sure that the learning is distilled, providing absolute lucidity for the class teacher about what the essential priorities for teaching are. Sharing the knowledge organisers with students is also extremely powerful: they then know what they will need to remember to do well in that particular topic.

The Individual Lesson

So, we have broken down our planning schedules: we have the telescopic yearly overview, confidence in our understanding of subject content and our streamlined knowledge organisers. These plans mean that we have a seamless transition between lessons, and the individual lesson content is informed by this overall sense of direction. All of these will ultimately save us both time and anxiety: we are in control over the direction of learning in our classrooms.

Our focus in the individual lesson will be to streamline the learning for students, to simplify the delivery and avoid both cognitive overload and multitasking. We will also consciously avoid the notion of an individual lesson being activity based, quickly transitioning between activities without any real learning goal. Instead, we will embrace what Peps Mccrea, in Lean Lesson Planning (2015), defines as 'the Shortest Path'. By consciously slowing down our thinking for the individual lesson experience, we instead prioritise the end point, considering the learning we want students to retain. Carl Hendrick and Robin Macpherson (2017) summarised what they learned from researching for their book on educational research:

One of the things we have learned in writing this book is that an awful lot of what goes on in the classroom simply doesn't matter. The signal-to-noise ratio is often at a less than optimal level for effective learning, with many extraneous activities taking up valuable learning time in the name of demonstrating progress, whether that be burdensome marking strategies or the creation of time-consuming resources to engage students. Many of these approaches not only have a limited impact on learning but they can have a hugely detrimental impact on teacher workload and teacher wellbeing.

There is a need for us to leave behind the desire to overly complicate learning in our classrooms. As Henry Thoreau (1908) highlights: 'our life is frittered away by detail. Simplify, simplify, simplify'. This is an adage that is wonderfully applicable to lessons. Lesson time is often 'frittered away', so our mission with the individual lesson is to keep the purpose, clarity and direction as streamlined as possible.

While each of the following planning principles will be expanded on throughout *Slow Teaching*, our individual lesson planning should ideally encompass the following:

Step 1: Ascertaining prior knowledge
Lessons should invest heavily in checking students' understanding from previous weeks; on recalling and remembering what has come before. Without being confident of this, we are effectively guessing what the direction of our lesson will be. The opening of the lesson is the optimal moment to begin this review. Barak Rosenshine (2012) states that 'The most effective teachers in the studies of classroom instruction understood the importance of practice, and they began their lessons with a five-to-eight-minute review of previously covered material'.

Step 2: Student thinking
Our planning for lessons needs to reflect carefully on what it is we want students to be thinking about at each stage of the lesson. In Daniel Willingham's (2009) view 'learning is the residue of thought'. This is a careful distinction between what students are actively doing, as this does not necessarily result in them thinking and engaging with their learning. Tasks should be designed with careful consideration about how we manage our students' thinking process throughout the lesson.

Step 3: Guided success
Clarity around exactly what our expectations of students are, and what we want them to produce in our lessons, is vital. In our planning stage, we need to consider how we will guide students towards being able to produce a final outcome. Deconstructing modelled examples with students, talking through our own thought process, and breaking down the skills, are all steps that need to be included if we want students to develop a sense of clarity about the expectations we have for them.

Step 4: Deliberate practice
Planning will be at its most effective if we also give students time to practice independently the skills we want them to gain confidence in. This practice enables students to repeat tasks over lessons and weeks, in order to ensure clarity of understanding and mastery of the skills. This is another justification for why the slow unit planning is vital: these moments of deliberate practice need to planned for periodically. Brown *et al* (2014) note that 'The striving, failure, problem solving and renewed attempts that characterise deliberate practice build the new knowledge, physiological adaptions, and complex mental models required to attain ever high levels'.

Step 5: Check for understanding
The best teachers frequently plan for moments that will check their students' comprehension of material throughout individual lessons. Without doing this, we have no real understanding of what is and what isn't working in our classroom. As we work through *Slow Teaching*, we will see the various strategies we can use to facilitate this – the most obvious being the use of questioning.

Maximising Planning Time

Albert Einstein (a man whose guidance on planning we should heed) said, in response to a question about what he would do given one hour to save the world, 'I would spend forty-five minutes defining the problem and only five minutes finding the solution'. Planning must be towards the top of our teaching hierarchy of needs: it should be the means by which we spend a significant amount of our time outside of teaching lessons. Otherwise, Mr Hare's myopic philosophy begins to work its way back into our daily life in school.

Planning is our framework for teaching, a vital process to help us to provide the best for our students. Yet, it will only go so far, unless we can secure positive relationships with them. We shall return to this integral area once we have welcomed in our intrepid youngsters – who will be the fruits of our systematic and excellent planning – into our streamlined environment. Before we begin to inspire and challenge them with our wonderful subjects, it is time to consider how we use our non-verbal communication.

Slow Questions

1. Are you falling into the Mr Hare planning trap?

2. Do you have a clear vision of where each class you teach needs to be by the end of the term and by the end of the year?

3. Have you broken down the learning into manageable chunks of planning?

4. Do you have a clear idea of what each assessment will be for schemes of work?

5. Have you slowly mastered the content you will be teaching?

6. Have you considered student misconceptions in your planning?

7. Have you planned for slow and deliberate practice in individual lessons?

8. Are you regularly checking your students' understanding?

CHAPTER 4:
AN ACTOR'S PARADISE:
THE NON-VERBAL IN
THE CLASSROOM

Electric communication will never be a substitute for the face of someone who with their soul encourages another person to be brave and true.
Charles Dickens

Please hold in your mind for a moment a public speaker you admire. It may be a figure who has influenced your desire to take on what some might argue is the most demanding of public speaking roles: a teacher. Now, examine the way they use their bodies, hands and facial expressions. Watch how they hold themselves gracefully in order to radiate conviction and generate a positive impression. Note the movements that act in sync with their words to make communication appear effortless. There is something mesmerising; a gravitas and control they have that gives an audience trust and confidence in their words.

Public Speaking: Nature or Nurture?

For me, the speaker I admire most is the former US president Barack Obama, a man who many believe mastered the art of public speaking with conviction. It is interesting to reflect on how Obama's body language developed over his political career. His hesitant first recorded speech, from 1995, challenges simplistic generalisations that good public speaking is a skill we are gifted with. Later, when he burst onto the scene at the Democratic National Convention in 2004, his speech was characterised by extensive supporting hand gestures. He pointed frequently and used his hands to reiterate his core messages, supporting his aim of conveying energy and dynamism. Fast-forward ten years and you see a much more stately and restrained presence, with his body language befitting of his position of president. He rarely gesticulates, and uses his hands in considered ways to support what he is saying.

The evolution of Obama's non-verbal communication is an example of how mastering effective body language on the public stage can be learned and crafted with deliberate practice. For our purposes, reflecting carefully on the way we employ our gestures and movement in the classroom can have a real impact in cultivating that mythical quality: teacher presence.

The Influence of Body Language

In our role in school we often have thousands of interactions each day. Many of these are verbal, but we often employ an array of non-verbal and silent signals to accompany our words. These microexpressions register immediately with the students in our classrooms, with long-lasting implications in the development of effective relationships and the efficacy of learning. As Carol Kinsey Goman (2011) argues 'all our efforts to communicate effectively can be derailed by even the smallest non-verbal gestures'.

Consider the scene: it is period five on a Friday. It has been a long week; you are tired, fractured and irritable. Your shoulders are hunched, arms are crossed and a hand is placed in front of your mouth. The class can sense tension and anxiety, it is clear that you are radiating irritability. They feed off this energy and the inevitable result ensues: a long, difficult lesson in which time slows to a grinding halt.

No matter how much experience we have, we are all familiar with this scenario. When we experience certain emotions, our bodies are our physical mirrors. It can be very challenging to hide this in front of thirty searching eyes. So, how could this scene have been different? What silent strategies can we put in place to facilitate a sense of calm ownership and to influence a more positive reception?

The Power of Posture

Perhaps the easiest place to begin is the way we hold ourselves: our posture.

Social psychologist Amy Cuddy's popular TED talk *Your body language may shape who you are* (2015) argued that there was scientific evidence behind her theory of power posing: how standing or sitting a certain way even just for two minutes has a transferable impact on testosterone levels and lowers the stress hormone cortisol. What the popularity of this talk and her subsequent book – *Presence: Bringing Your Boldest Self to Your Biggest Challenge* (2016) – highlight is that we are aware of the power of body language and conscious that we would like to be able to use it to improve perception of us. Yet, what it also illustrates is our desire for quick solutions, a speedy 'fix' that can alter how people respond to us.

A series of follow-up studies appear to suggest that there is no scientific basis to Cuddy's arguments. Indeed, one of her research collaborators issued a statement highlighting she does 'not believe the power pose effects are real' and 'the evidence against the existence of power poses is undeniable' (Carney, 2016).

Whether or not holding a 'pose' has any long-term benefits, adopting good posture can positively impact our own confidence, and can influence the opinion that students might have of us. By working to develop improved posture, we also begin to alleviate the symptoms that can often appear married to teaching: that irritating tension and pain in the neck, shoulders and back. It also influences how much of a presence we have at the front of the room, giving our instructions a greater sense of clarity and purpose.

Research has indicated that the more we adopt an upright posture, the more we can maintain our self-esteem, reduce negative moods and increase positivity in comparison to a slumped posture. Importantly, in the teaching profession, good posture also increases our self-focus and capacity to communicate well.

However, there remains the question: how exactly do we improve it?

Effective Posture

What is good posture? Well, it certainly isn't standing rigidly and uncomfortably, becoming the teaching equivalent of the Tin Man. Obviously, it is also a rejection of the sloucher: that flopped fish that inspires the frequent reminders that we give students in our classrooms about sitting up straight.

Primarily, good posture is about maintaining a relaxed upright appearance and a neutral spine: being alert, but not stiff. Ideally, we should aim to follow the three contours of the spine, working to ensure the ears, shoulders, hips, knees and ankles align in one straight line. This will enable us to follow the spine's natural curvature, with our necks' straight and shoulders parallel with the hips. The head should remain centred over the shoulders and extended up towards the ceiling. To break this down more, it is useful to consider how we stand at the front of the classroom.

The Stance

As a focus and visual point for students, our posture is perhaps most important when we are standing at the front of the room. In 'Ted Talks: The Official TED guide to public speaking' Chris Anderson (2017) gives the following guidance about how to present oneself at the front of a room:

> The simplest way to give a talk powerfully is just to stand tall, putting equal weight on both feet, which are positioned comfortably a few inches apart... This mode can project calm authority. Good posture helps; avoid slouching your shoulders forward.

Begin by finding your centre, aiming to achieve alignment and balance at the front of the room. Feet should be shoulder width apart, with weight resting on the balls of your feet. Then, square your shoulders and pull up your head and chin. This posture is also useful for assisting us to breathe well and to project our voices effectively. As Patsy Rodenburg (2015) notes, 'The natural way of standing is based on achieving balance, ease and feeling control'.

By finding this sense of poise and remaining static, you are ready to convey seamless confidence and have young people absorbing your every comment and instruction. You are also more likely to curb some of those individual 'quirks' that can have the impact of distracting young people. Standing in this manner also means we resist the urge to stand with crossed arms, a posture that is typically used to convey displeasure and can impact how students respond to us.

Building Routines

However focussed we may be initially on secure good posture, they often tend to easily (metaphorically and physically) slouch. There will need to be frequent internal reminders in order to remind yourself when standing at the front of the class: this could be a repeated adage such as 'stand tall and square shoulders'. If you prefer a visual image, you can always think about your body being held up by a long piece of string, pulling you gently up towards the ceiling. Another trick is to associate posture with an object or colour; every time you recall that object, use it as a posture reminder. The important point is that improved posture will not happen in isolation. Reminders and frequent checking will be required to assist you in securing long term ballet-style posture!

The Seating Slump

Having stood and projected our wisdom for hours throughout the day, the natural temptation is to collapse the moment we can rest our weary legs, often face first into a pile of books. Yet this has the reverse effect, making us feel lethargic and demotivated and increasing our stress levels.

Instead, when sitting, the ideal posture to adopt is to sustain a straight back and shoulder blades. Aiming to be sitting against the back of the chair will provide a helping hand to remaining straight. Those pesky feet will desperately try to move: keep them flat on the floor and your elbows flat on the table. This will help to keep your shoulders relaxed. The key is to have your head as straight as possible, avoiding tilting the chin down towards the chest. Importantly, if you are sitting for a long time, try to take regular breaks in order to stand and stretch; this will sustain the new straight sitting philosophy!

It takes conscious, deliberate and frequent effort to improve posture. You are effectively training your muscles to work against what may have been years of poor posture. It requires a steely voice of perseverance that urges you to retrain those muscles that will initially scream at you in awkward defiance.

Hand Gestures

Teachers do not need to be told that young people are easily distracted. We know that we will have their attention stolen from us by the most miniscule of interruptions. Yet, at times, we can be our own worst enemies, diverting students' attention away from the lesson through our own behaviours and characteristics in the classroom. Our hands, in this respect, can be our greatest ally or our most sworn enemy.

Some teachers are wildly eccentric with their hand gestures, embracing the airport marshall approach and gesticulating in ways that can only serve to distract students. As a classroom teacher, you can see this occur when children hypnotically watch our hands rather than listening to anything we are saying. Alongside this, it is easy to misinterpret hand gestures, which can result in confusion regarding instructions that have been given by the teacher to students. At times we can become overwhelmed by our enthusiasm and passion, and this can be reflective in our body language, often resulting in classes mirroring this erratic lack of control in their own behaviours.

However, the contrast of the airport marshall – the robot – is just as harmful. A static hand user communicates both a lack of passion for their subject and a lack of warmth towards their audience. Any sense of indifference is certainly not what we want to promote in the classroom.

The middle ground to these contrasting approaches comes from slowing down hand gestures and eliminating distracting mannerisms to naturally amplify what we are saying. This will sustain the enthusiasm we have for our subject and help us to convey sincerity. It is, of course, about finding ways in which we are most comfortable and natural, but recognising that using our hands in certain ways can help to encourage learning means that we can learn to use them effectively.

Purposeful Gestures

In an ideal world our hand gestures should help us to be as convincing as possible for our students.. Keeping the hands unlocked throughout the teaching day means we avoid tightly compressed and constrained body language styles. It also means we avoid the 'fidget teaching' trap, speaking while waving a pen around in front of us.

It is useful to first undergo a body language self-assessment. Asking a colleague to pop into a lesson for ten minutes to give you some body language pointers is very helpful. (It can be difficult to take an objective look at how we present ourselves in the classroom without this help.) If you have access to a video recorder, film yourself teaching. This is a very useful (if, initially, rather disconcerting) process that provides an authentic student perception of how we present ourselves.

Smooth and restrained gestures arguably work best when they amplify the points we are making. By slowing down our gestures, we slow down the quality of our words. Sustaining a hand gesture for a few seconds can help to hold the concentration of students in the room. They can also be used to dramatise the points and ideas we are making, or to encourage more participation from our students.

Eye Contact

Connection in the classroom is vitally important. Unconsciously, we have the ability to generate scepticism, boredom and incomprehension if we don't form positive relationships with our students. There is also the danger of falling into the 'content trap': becoming so focused on delivering the material that we forget to engage with the students who are in front of us. Common sense applies here – as adults, would we really listen to anyone who didn't engage with us through eye contact while they spoke? James Borg (2004) has suggested that 'Increasing eye contact has a positive effect. It can show that you're attentive, that you like somebody and that you're sincere'. One of the easiest ways to help create classrooms built on a mutual rapport is through meaningful eye contact; it helps to build both credibility and trust with our students.

Michael Marland's guide on eye contact, from the classic text *The Craft of the Classroom* (1993), is particularly helpful:

The key is communication with your eyes. Feel the sectors of the room and underline the structure and sequence of your remarks by directing phrases to the different sectors... Within each group, look only at one pupil, a different one each time you return to the sector, and cast your remark to him.

I often find myself guilty of tunnel vision when communicating with a class, looking only at a small proportion of the students in front of me or scanning the room quickly while I talk. The contrast to this is not about labouring eye contact directly to one student while the rest of the class get up to all kinds of mischief, it is about being more thoughtful about who is receiving eye contact. Importantly, it is about sustaining three to five seconds of eye contact with students to make them feel more included and invested in the lesson. We can then check how responsive they are to our messaging and how focused they are in their learning. We are also improving their concentration, removing the chances of passivity, at best, and apathy, at worst. One of the vital behaviour management strategies is the insistence of all eyes on you – this becomes easier to demand when we ourselves are meeting the eyes of all our students in the room.

Purposeful Movement

There is an oft-repeated claim about body language that is hugely misleading but that, nonetheless, continues to be used to further arguments. It comes from research carried out by Professor Albert Mahrabian (1981) who suggested in his book, *Silent Messages*, that only seven percent of the effectiveness of communication is down to language, while 38% depends on tone of voice and 55% comes from body language. What those who use this to support training on body language conveniently avoid, however, is the fact that these experiments focused only on how *emotion* is communicated. There is even a rejoinder on Pr. Mahrabian's website, stating: 'Please note that this and other equations regarding relative importance of verbal and nonverbal messages were derived from experiments dealing with communications of feelings and attitudes' (See: www.kaaj.com/psych/smorder.html).

Yet, a huge amount of our movements in the classroom are indeed about communicating emotion and expectations. To try to place a definitive rule on how to employ movement in the classroom would be ludicrous. Perhaps what we may wish to reflect on as a guiding principle would be calm, assertive and intentional movement. Chris Anderson (2017) touches on this issue:

Something to avoid is nervously shifting from leg to leg or walking forward and back a couple of steps in a kind of rocking motion... So move if you want to. But if you do move, move intentionally. And then, when you want to emphasise a point, stop and address your audience from a stance of quiet power.

When we are anxious and tense, our movement in the room betrays this emotion: we move in jerky ways, we fidget and we pace up and down. Deliberately slowing down the way we move around the room will feel unnatural at first, yet what it will project is both control and confidence.

Ownership

How can we communicate our sense of ownership over our classrooms? Partly, it is about our ability to move beyond the narrow confinements of the front of the room. Doug Lemov (2010) calls this technique 'break[ing] the plane':

> The "plane" of your classroom is the imaginary line that runs the length of the room, parallel to and about five feet in front of the board... Some teachers are hesitant or slow to "break the plane" – to move past this imaginary barrier and out among the desks and rows.

The subliminal message this purposeful movement sends to students is powerful: it shows both our sense of control and our desire to be alongside them in their learning. Motivation actually stems from the Latin 'to move', and the movements we make in the classroom can have a huge influence on how engaged and interested our students are.

Strategic Circulation

We spend a significant amount of lesson time circulating the room: it is how we maintain positive behaviour, root out students' misconceptions and check their understanding. But, often, circulating the room can turn into casual wandering that is without purpose and meaning.

Demystifying the reason why room circulation occurs is one useful way to give it more value. Providing a rationale for how long we will circulate the classroom, and what exactly we are looking for, will give our movement a greater sense of purpose and direction. Real engagement with individuals (including literally being down on their level) while we circulate can do wonders for motivation and focus in the room.

There is no doubt that there is a distinct element of performance involved in the craft of the classroom teacher. The adage about teachers as actors has more than a grain of truth. We are immensely visual throughout the day; it is one of the most tiring aspects of the role. Hopefully the silent strategies that we have armed ourselves with in this chapter will go some way towards using our presence to its full potential. Now that we are oozing gravitas and conviction from our body language, it is time for us to approach the most obvious form of communication: how we talk in the classroom.

Slow Questions

1. Do you spend time reflecting on your non-verbal communication in the classroom?

2. Are you conscious of your posture and the impact it has?

3. Could you embrace a straighter, more upright posture?

4. Do you use hand gestures purposefully to support your words?

5. Do you have teacher blind spots in the classroom; are you engaging with the whole room through eye contact?

6. How could you use eye contact more effectively to build positive relationships?

7. Could you move more strategically in your classroom?

PART II: SLOW TALK

CHAPTER 5: EFFICIENT TEACHER TALK

The upshot of what I have to say is this: I am telling you to be a slow-speaking person.
Seneca

The philosopher Seneca devoted the last three years of his life to exchanging a series of letters with Lucilius Junior. In one letter, young Lucilius makes the mistake of confessing his admiration for another philosopher, Serapio, saying that 'his words tend to be tumbled out at a tremendous pace, pounded and driven along rather than poured out, for they come in a volume no one voice could cope with'. A horrified Seneca delivers an impressive rejection: 'This copious and impetuous energy in a speaker is better suited to a hawker, than to someone who deals with a subject of serious importance and is also a teacher'. He continues to note the 'great deal of futility and emptiness about this style of speaking, which has more noise about it than effectiveness' (Seneca, 2003).

How much of Seneca's advice is still relevant today? How many times are we asked to slow down or repeat ourselves when launching into quick instructions, or talking at the front of the class? How often do we return at the end of a working day exhausted, unable to draw up the vocal energy to communicate with our loved ones?

The Importance of Teacher Talk

For some time in education there would be audible gasps of shock if teacher talk dared to appear in a conversation about how best young people learn. The mere mention of the term Direct Instruction (the explicit teaching of a skill set) would lead to scoffed response about the danger of becoming a 'sage on the stage'. Or there would be quips about being a didactic lecturer to a room full of 'vaults', as parodied by Thomas Gradgrind in *Hard Times*: 'Now, what I want is Facts. Teach these boys and girls nothing but Facts. Facts alone are wanted in life. Plant nothing else, and root out everything else' (Dickens, 1995).

Instead, facts and knowledge appeared to be rejected in the drive to silence the teacher. Myths about young peoples' capacity to learn and retain information

49

dominated: they could not possibly listen to more than two minutes of teacher talk at a time. Instead, 'fast' learning methods dominated: collaborative classroom strategies, enquiry-based learning and accelerated learning. The teacher facilitated such work, but to lead in this respect was to error. Ofsted and political agendas added fuel to the dousing of talk, promoting the 'guide on the side' approach to teaching and depicting real learning as 'fun' and 'engaging'.

To provide the minimal instruction in the classroom, however, may be doing our students a disservice. As Richard E. Clark *et al* (2012) have noted 'Decades of research clearly demonstrate that *for novices* (comprising virtually all students), direct, explicit instruction is more effective and more efficient than partial guidance.' Expecting students to discover learning for themselves, without necessary input from teachers, leads to misconceptions that are left unchallenged.

Thankfully, we have come a long way from both the didacticism of Gradgrind and his Victorian ilk, and more modern progressive learning theories. Recent research such as the above from Richard E Clark, alongside the voices of dissenting teachers, has started to see more of a thoughtful approach. There is a movement away from muting teachers in the classroom to a much more meaningful dialogue: what exactly is efficient and effective teacher talk?

The Pace of Speech

Initially, our priority is to remember what Edward de Bono (1999) notes: 'communication is always understood in the context and experience of the receiver – no matter what was intended'. In this respect, it is important to remember that young people find it challenging to process huge amounts of information. Their days involve moving between classrooms, and adapting to different subjects and methods of explaining. Lessons are most overwhelming for these learning 'tourists' when we fall into the 'racing through content' trap; that is, when we speak quickly and couple our verbal information with huge amounts of written slides on a PowerPoint.

When we deliver instructions, we often rush through it, requiring our students to work very hard to sustain their focus. It strains their working memories; that is, their capacity to retain additional information in their minds. Working memories are not yet fully formed in adolescence, meaning that students are more likely to forget aspects of instructions before the sequence of guidance has been completely presented to them.

As we are all too well aware, exerting additional effort is just not in some young peoples' skill-set. If we want to develop their capacity to retain information and listen, then altering the speed of how we deliver this information is one of our starting points. It is also the first step in the masterful teacher skill of making complex ideas seem remarkably simple and easy to grasp.

There will, however, be times when we want to speed up what we are saying in the classroom, and to argue that we should always sustain a specific speed while speaking would be ludicrous. To maintain a repetitive drone would be a sure way to ensure inattentive and frustrated students. When we regale students with anecdotes, or wildly convey our enthusiasm for the beauty of a particular piece of poetry (just me?), we will want to speed up, to inject the sense of urgency and passion we feel. Speaking quickly at this point is important. We don't need them to retain everything we are saying, but we want to make sure we are connecting with them emotionally and sustaining their attention.

Reflecting on Explanations

Reflecting on how we speak in our classrooms is a vital starting point. Patsy Rodenburg (2015) urges her readers to record a section of their speech to give them a clearer insight into how quickly they speak. As she points out, 'Many fast or slow speakers are positively startled when they first hear the pace of their speech on tape... The person then begins to realise how hard it is for listeners to follow them'.

Ben Newmark, a history teacher who has written extensively on improving explanations and runs a YouTube revision website for his students, highlights that we are prone to the 'illusory superiority' – the belief that we communicate with more skill than, perhaps, we may have. He remembers how disconcerting recording his own explanations was: 'I was no better than OK. I said "um" a lot. I overused the word "right". I said everything was 'a really important point' (Newmark, 2017). Having this objective view of our own speech is vital and helps us to refine and improve our communication, particularly when it comes to explaining more demanding content.

Processing for Complex Material

A significant amount of what we do as educators is explain complex things to young people in the hope they will understand, recall and remember. These are the moments in which we need our students to grasp a troublesome concept, to recall a particular definition, or to be secure in a piece of knowledge. Chip and Dan Heath (2007) have suggested an interesting mnemonic to assist in securing knowledge – SUCCES: 'simple, unexpected, concrete, credible, emotional and story'. A final element in ensuring knowledge can be both accessed and remembered, is the *pace* in which we deliver the material.

Usually, we deliver 130-170 words per minute at a natural conversational speed. When we want to introduce key ideas or explain challenging concepts that will be vital to the students' understanding, it requires us to deliberately alter from our natural speed to a more measured pace.

An interesting example of this is Martin Luther King's 'I Have a Dream' speech. King's delivery throughout was at around 100 words per minute. That, coupled with his use of repetition (more on that later), meant that the speech is among the most memorable in history. It was beautifully crafted for impact, delivered to achieve maximum purpose and had a memorable and resounding theme of unity.

Slowing down to achieve a similar impact in our explanations and instruction requires real confidence and preparation. It is challenging to think about both what we are saying *and* how we are saying it. It requires pre-planned explanations that encompass the slow rhythm and cadence of oratory.

Winston Churchill was arguably the greatest of slow preparers and certainly not the most natural of public speakers. As a child he suffered from a lisp and stammered, vowing that one of his 'only ambition[s] was to be master of the spoken word' (Leaming, 2011). For him, preparation was everything; he often wrote out his speeches word for word (apparently an hour for every minute!) and wrote endless drafts. For Churchill, 'preparation is, if not the key to being a genius, then at least the key to sounding like a genius' (Leaming, 2010).

To explain something well we need to have concrete and secure subject knowledge, as well as empathy in order to appreciate the misconceptions students might have. While we may not want to fully embrace Churchillian degrees of preparation, we do want to ensure that we have invested time in scripting out and practising our classroom talk. As Peps Mccrea (2017) states, 'To improve the leanness of our communication, we must first get crystal clear about the idea we are trying to convey'.

We also need to make sure that the atmosphere in the room mirrors this calm and thoughtful approach when we want to deliver an explanation. Basic, but often forgotten, aspects of delivery are important. The first is explaining what we are about to say will be useful and vital for our students; rationalising why we need them to listen attentively. This is coupled with having the confidence to wait until we have the undivided attention from all the students in the room. We will need to actively teach and model to students how to listen appropriately: with eye contact and guiding them to have their hands free from any distractions essential. Slowing down what we say will then give impetus to the instruction; they will recognise that they have to carefully listen in order to ensure their understanding.

Achieving a More Measured Pace

One good technique to avoid speaking too quickly is to pick out key words to slow down on when speaking to the class. These might be essential subject-specific words or key points in the instruction – points we need our students to be completely clear on.

Then it is about becoming more mindful about how we are breathing when speaking at the front of the room. Often when we are tense and speaking quickly, our breathing speeds up. Slowing down our breathing will allow us to become more self-aware about the pace of our explanations. Learning to read the faces in the room while we deliver information will also assist us in recognising how we are using our voices. Our students become mirrors of our pace: if we see eyes glaze over, we are going too quickly; if we witness a sea of yawning, the likelihood is we are going too slowly.

The next step is about savouring and enunciating vowels and consonants in words, fully pronouncing vital words and elongating them in order to accentuate their meaning. Experimenting with how we can sustain the classes' attention when we drop the pace is also important; again, we will be able to note when they are drifting.

Mastering the Pause

Writing without punctuation is remarkably difficult to follow, and speech without pauses inspires exactly the same emotions: frustration and confusion. The pause in a classroom is, therefore, our manner of punctuating clearly what we are saying for emphasis. Often, however, in our rush to convey information or secure the attention of young people, we miss out on opportunities for reflection. Valerie Coultas (2007) has highlighted teachers' reluctance to pause, advising us 'not [to] rush into speech. Less experienced teachers often fail to understand the importance of pauses and silence and the contribution these moments make to the classroom atmosphere'.

The first rationale for the pause is self-explanatory: it gives our students the chance to catch up with us in their cognitive processing. When a pause is well timed, it can ensure that they are following our points and gives them time to process content. A scan of the room, or a quick question-and-answer session, allows us to gather awareness of our students and informs us if we need to hold back, so as to ensure that they have all grasped the explanations or instructions.

The pause for emphasis on important words is another way to ensure that students can recognise that we are delivering important instructions. This might be a particularly troublesome topic or word that we want students to recall and remember.

Pausing can also embody confidence and composure: another passport to teacher gravitas. Achieving the required effect is simple: take a deep breath and inhale to three. This can be coupled with making the pause explicit for students, informing them that there will be a moment to allow them to think carefully about the content. At this stage we are also demonstrating to students that taking time to think is a vital part of developing understanding and independence in learning.

Pitch It

How we use the pitch of our voice when communicating with students also influences how attentive they are and how much they will remember. When considering using different pitches, there are two aspects to avoid: losing pitch volume towards the end of a sentence (falling off the line) and going down at the end of each sentence (dipping). To avoid this, it is important to sustain the vocal energy from start to finish in a sentence. If we visualise the last word in a sentence, we will also give it more energy and help give our voices more clarity.

It is also important to avoid vocal monotony: speaking at the same high nasal pitch. As teachers we can be guilty of this when we want to dominate the room and make sure that our students can hear nothing but our voices. One way to address this is to modify our tone often in our communication, thus energising our speaking.

Redundant Speech

There is a treasure trove of phrases used in the classroom that are redundant and repetitive. Repetition for emphasis has its place, but streamlining our teacher communication is also vitally important. My repetitive quirks are the following: OK, folks and listen. I know that I mindlessly repeat them in lessons (the 'folks' tally is particularly dangerous!) The more self-aware we are about our tendency to repeat such words, the more we can compress our language into its bare essentials and explain things clearly.

Eliminating fillers in our instructions is particularly important: we are striving to model excellent speaking for our students to mirror, so maintaining a formal and clear style of our own is important. Fillers serve to detract from the main purpose of speaking, meaning that it is easier to lose the thread of what is being explained. Instead of using fillers, getting into the habit of replacing them with a pause can help our students to follow content and model good speaking habits.

Repetition

To return to our philosophers, Aristotle described learning by saying 'it is frequent repetition that produces a natural tendency.' We already seen our philosophical friends had some sage guidance, so repetition of key subject specific terminology is a useful starting point. To guide students on how to use subject-specific vocabulary well, we need to ensure that we are frequently repeating and reminding them of key phrases in our own instructions and explanations. This will require us to repeat definitions slowly and ask students to repeat these along with us; there is nothing like some unison whole-class chanting to help imbed an important fact or definition. Also useful is our own signposting of repetition: making it very clear that we have repeated something important. Our knowledge organisers are an excellent way for us to distil the essential points we need for a unit and ensure that students have grasped the important points.

Spaced repetition of content is another important way of ensuring students can retain information. Information must be recalled and repeated to ensure it is secure in our students' long-term memory. This might require us to repeat explanations, skilfully altering the language we use to try to build in more familiarity for our students.

Storytelling

Humans have a tradition of oral storytelling for one reason: people are captivated and intrigued by the power of a story. It binds us together and builds relationships and intimacy. Daniel Willingham (2010) argues that stories have immense value in supporting memory. As he notes, 'The human mind seems exquisitely tuned to understand and remember stories – so much so that psychologists sometimes refer to stories as "psychologically privileged"'.

Instead of racing into delivering content immediately, considering how we could create intrigue and interest by building the content of a story may have significant impact in encouraging retention. Planning in advance how the story could be sculpted to encourage students' interest will help to generate mystery around a topic. The story itself also needs to be sparse, as 'formal work in laboratory settings has shown that people rate stories as less interesting if they include too much information, thus leaving no inferences for the listener to make' (Willingham, 2010).

It is not just the story that can build more emotional engagement and interest for our students; an anecdote from our own experience can spark a similar hook that resonates with young people. Shaun Allison and Andy Tharby (2015) have described the humanising factor of this approach, stating that:

> Some students find it difficult to believe that teachers are living, breathing human beings with personal lives beyond the classroom. Anecdotes from teachers' lives fascinate them, especially if these titbits of information are drip-fed over time.

Deviating from the formal style of instruction by including an anecdote can breathe life and drama into a topic and engage students. It makes what we are teaching meaningful, bringing our students into our world and facilitating more positive relationships.

Curbing Teacher Talk

We have seen in this chapter that teacher talk is valuable, but only when it is streamlined and carefully employed. Importantly, at times it also needs to be stopped completely. There can be a tendency to provide an elaborate narration to all aspects of the classroom, to disjoint young people's thinking by talking over them endlessly. Embracing silence and muting ourselves regularly can help to ensure that students are actively thinking, and can save teachers much needed energy. This is most obviously required when students are working independently. This is the time when they need to have ultimate focus, so as to be able translate the dialogue and instructions they have received into meaningful output. Rather than interrupting their thinking process by loudly delivering general corrections or instructions, at this point we are best served by letting them practise independently.

Quality explanations, instructions and the pace at which we speak are clearly all vital. However, how we employ these aspects of teaching needs to be carefully planned so that we involve the individuals who share our space with us. We are not on a stage delivering some magnificent soliloquy. Talk needs to be interactive, to engage our students, to check that they can understand exactly what we sharing with them. As Graham Nuthall (2007) notes, most students already know 50% of the information they are taught. Instruction by itself will not lead us to discover what students already know. Time to step tentatively into the murky and complex world of questioning...

Slow Questions

1. Could your teacher talk be deliberately slowed down?

2. Are you aware of your breathing in the classroom and how this is impacting your ability to explain?

3. Could you embrace elements of the Churchillian preparation of your teacher talk?

4. Are you aware of how students are responding to the pace of your speech?

5. What could you do to employ the pause more effectively in the classroom?

6. Are you harnessing the power of slow storytelling and anecdotes in the classroom?

CHAPTER 6: QUESTIONING: REDISCOVERING THE POTENTIAL

A prudent question is one half of wisdom.
Frances Bacon

As teachers we fully embrace Albert Einstein's famous 'never stop questioning' philosophy: we question students like the 'stuttering rifles' rapid rattle' in Wilfred Owen's poem 'Anthem for Doomed Youth' (1917). It is a vital part of our teaching practice; we are likely to fire out hundreds of question in any given school day and employ thousands of them throughout the week (questions, not rifles!) The automatic 'rapid rattle' approach to questioning, however, often results in losing a great degree of its value in our classrooms.

The Value of Questioning

What exactly does our brain do when we hear a question and what impact does this have on learning? Richard W. Paul and Linda Elder (2000) have suggested that:

> Thinking is not driven by answers but by questions. Had no questions been asked by those who laid the foundation for a field, for example Physics or Biology, the field would never have developed in the first place... To think or rethink anything, one must ask questions that stimulate our thoughts.

Questions, therefore, become a significant ally in the mission to encourage active thinking from our students in the classroom. Ultimately, the brain can only focus on one thing at a time; therefore, the moment young people hear a question, they automatically begin to engage with it. Neuroscientist John Medina (2012) states that 'Research shows that we can't multitask. We are biologically incapable of processing attention-rich inputs simultaneously'. We exploit this by asking a question, ensuring that the attention is focused on the immediate question that has been asked. Importantly, there is also the motivation that questioning inspires – it gives our students active opportunities to participate in discussions and demonstrate their knowledge.

Questioning is also our way of checking the progress and comprehension of the students in our classroom, signalling to us whether we can move on with the material we are exploring. It is a vital way to explore their understanding of immediate lesson content or, when we are recapping and returning to topics, to see how much of it our students have retained. Barak Rosenshine (2012) argues that this is most effective when we seek to unpick how students arrived at a particular answer:

> Questions allow a teacher to determine how well the material has been learned and whether there is a need for additional instruction. The most effective teachers also ask students to explain the process they used to answer the question, to explain how the answer was found. Less successful teachers ask fewer questions and almost no process questions.

Another part of our educational mission is to increase students' capacity to think critically and improve their higher-order thinking skills. By doing this we are also developing their ability to engage philosophically with the world. Martin Robinson (2013) dubs this as aiming to produce philosopher kids. As he argues:

> In a true democracy all citizens share responsibility for their community. We need to educate all young people to be philosopher kids, to be part of the philosopher crowds, finding their way through the global village.

Modelling this behaviour and developing students' ability to have deep and intellectual exchanges in our classroom – a place in which new ideas and opinions are valued – will help students prepare for the world outside of school. Additionally, these skills will teach students to make sense of 'the global village'.

Questioning Traps

Due to the sheer volume of questions we ask throughout the working day, it is inevitable that we can begin to 'rattle' off questions mechanically, without the necessary reflection on how best to use them. The result is that even with the very best of intentions, we can find ourselves stumbling into some of the questioning traps. Interestingly, a great number are speed related:

Guess what is in the head: In our content-rich curriculum, we often feel the need to rush through material and specifications. We frequently ask questions that merely seek to reinforce the knowledge and content we have shared. We often do it without providing any insight into how our students are expected to answer the question. Questioning in this vein is merely encouraging young people to regurgitate the information we are looking for, with no real intellectual engagement. Those students who have the knowledge will volunteer, and the rest will switch off. Often, this can take the form of a rhetorical question that does not require a response or, even more tragically, we begin to answer our own questions without allowing for any time to hear responses.

Closed questions dominating: A large number of questions teachers ask require students to recall the facts and only test lower-order skills. George Brown and E. C. Wragg (2001) point out that higher-level questions are used in the classroom only 10 to 20% of the time. Ultimately, these questions lead to only single-word answers or a short factual response; they do not require any real degree of further explanation. While all questions have their place in the classroom, the dominance of closed questions is concerning. Are we doing enough to extend and challenge thinking?

Time: Often, we launch out one of our hundreds of questions and pounce immediately on the student who shows the first sign of response. The reality is that, on average, we allow only one second for our students to reflect on questions. If we pause to consider the internal process that they must go through in order to generate a response, this becomes even more troublesome. P. H. Winne and R. W. Marx (1983) note that students must 'perceive the instructional stimuli, note their occurrence, understand the cognitive processes that are required, use the processes to create or manipulate information to be stored as learned material and encode the information for later retrieval'. All this in one second? By not allowing sufficient time for student reflection, a significant number of students will give up and not go through this process, waiting instead for one of their more willing chums to take the lead.

Any questions? At various points in a lesson, we are often tempted to ask the students if anyone has any questions. We know that encouraging them to ask questions will aid learning and motivation. However, the majority of students are usually unwilling to admit publicly that they are unsure about the content. Would we, as adults, be willing to do the same in a room of our peers? Therefore, the silence we are greeted with leads us to assume that the knowledge is nestled beautifully inside their minds – an assumption that is untested and untried, and likely to be false. We move on too quickly, leaving an unknown proportion of the class uncertain about exactly what they should know or be doing next.

Acceptance: In our desire to motivate our students, we can often accept answers to questions that are overly simplistic or, indeed, wrong. As the next chapter on praise will evaluate, we often have the tendency to afford more positivity than an answer deserves, or we move on without probing further or seeking to refine the quality of answers.

Awareness of these traps can make us more thoughtful about how we employ questions. The following techniques can also ensure we maximise its potential in our teaching.

Recognition

How can we encourage more participation from students? What happens to these young idealists who ask endless questions as children, but go through adolescence being tentative and uncertain about volunteering answers?

There is an obvious way in which we can encourage more contribution. Very simply, it is about taking time to validate the efforts of young people, as they take the intimidating step to putting themselves forward to offer their thoughts publicly. Adolescence, as we will recall, is a time riddled with insecurity and doubt. As Doug Lemov (2015) states:

> To raise your hand is a critical act that deserves some reflection… In a micro-sense, every time students raise their hands, a milepost passes… To raise your hand is to mark the passage of an event worthy of action….

Volunteering to answer a question requires confidence: confidence in sharing ideas and in how they will be received by the class and teacher. If we, as teachers, recognise this effort positively and sincerely, then we will find that other students in the group seek to share more of their own answers. The converse is, as George Brown and E. C. Wragg (2001) highlight, that 'If children believe the teacher isn't interested in what they have to say, they will stop saying anything at all'. We are seeking to build an atmosphere of acceptance and community. If we fail to validate answers and effort, we begin to shatter not only the harmony in the group, but the confidence and desire of our students to share responses.

Validation Phases

The danger with validation is slipping into over-praise that exclaims 'fantastic', 'outstanding' and so on, in response to any incoherent grunt. Instead, the focus should be to recognise and value the thinking and effort that has taken place in the room. While it might not all have been the answers that we wanted to hear, it is the act of effort itself that we are seeking to encourage young people to do more of. The following phrases will recognise the answers we have heard, while keeping those who didn't get the opportunity to share their answers motivated:

'Thank you to all of those who have volunteered answers and thinking.'

'Clearly there is some real thinking going on in the room.'

'Lots of thoughtful and interesting comments and ideas, thank you for sharing.'

'Sorry we didn't hear from everyone in the room, keep thinking carefully and we will hear from you next time.'

Wait time

Before we unpick the style of the questions we ask, it is time to embrace the most obvious of the slow-teaching strategies: wait time. Mary Budd Rowe initially coined this phrase in 1972, when she identified the silence that teachers left at the end of questions as integral to improved learning. Her research found that the periods of silence between teacher questions and student responses rarely lasted more than a second and a half. When she explored the impact of raising this 'wait time' to at least three seconds, she discovered a range of benefits. Rowe (1987) later elaborated further, stating that:

> If teachers can increase the average length of the pauses at both points, namely, after a question and, even more importantly, after a student response to three seconds or more, there are pronounced changes in student use of language and logic.

Rowe discovered that there is a clear impact in the quality of discourse in the room when time was left for thinking ('wait time' was dubbed by Robert Stahl in 1985 as 'think time'). Importantly, it also impacts positively on student learning behaviours and on teacher skill sets. For students, the length and correctness of responses increased, the number of instances of the dreaded phrase 'I don't know' decreased, and volunteered answers increased. She discovered that as teachers build in more wait time, they become more thoughtful about the level of challenge in their questions and tend to employ more variable questioning strategies. The opposite of this – classrooms founded in quick responses with little time afforded for reflection – clearly feed superficial learning with responses left unchallenged and unrefined, resulting in fewer learning gains.

Wait time has many different applications; it is certainly not just to be used following a teacher's question. For each application, it is vital that teachers focus on students preserving the thinking silence:

1. **Teacher question:** Pose the question then pause, waiting for three to five seconds to hear feedback from students. Making it clear that you are waiting

for students to have further time for thinking is important when using this technique.

2. **During student responses:** Often, a student will pause and seek to clarify their thinking during responding to a question. We gasp in horror at the thought of a moment of silence in the lesson and interject. Allowing time will ensure the student can consider carefully without pressure, which is likely to improve the overall quality of the response.

3. **Post student response:** Slowing down at this point enables the other students to consider the response their classmate has given. This prevents teachers from leaping in to assess the quality of the answer, encouraging young people in the room to listen carefully and think about the response themselves. At this point we may consider asking students to reflect on the strengths and possible ways of developing the answer.

4. **General teacher wait time:** At times, we ourselves may need to take a moment to gather our thoughts and consider how we want to explain something or move the lesson forward. This is vital in modelling to students that thinking requires time, patience and deliberation.

Wait Phrases

'I want to give you some time to consider that question...'

'Think carefully about that idea for a moment...'

'Let's give ourselves some time to consider that thought...'

'What are our thoughts on that response?'

'How could we build on that interesting idea?'

'Can I ask you to pause and reflect on that idea?'

'Let's think about that for one moment...'

Preparation

A recurring theme throughout this book has been the investment of time in preparation. It is not about adding to our workload but, instead, about making informed and reflective decisions about our use of time, rather than mindless functioning. The notion of thoughtfully planning out the questions we will ask in lessons may well feel alien to us – surely we should be designing an outlandish PowerPoint or writing out streams of information?

The time invested in preparing questions, however, will be significant in assisting the learning of students in our rooms. It allows us to script out possible answers, giving us mastery over content and helping us to consider how we will differentiate our questioning appropriately in the classroom. While there must be room for spontaneous questioning, pre-planned questions can provide a guide to what exactly needs to be explored, adding to the sense of calm clarity about the direction of our lessons. Instead of using PowerPoint for lots of information, having a key question for the lesson on one slide can focus both our students and us on the central focus of the lesson.

Challenge

There is no right or wrong question to ask in the classroom; all are meaningful and useful in differing degrees. It is important, however, to balance our closed, factual questions that assess understanding with open questions that seek to challenge thinking. When we have established that the surface-level knowledge has been secured, we know then that we can embrace deeper and more conceptual questioning.

The shift to asking more challenging questions requires subtle alterations in our language so as to ensure that students build on points. Shaun Allison and Andy Tharby (2015) point out that 'A ladder is a useful metaphor: each question acts as a rung leading towards the core idea or concept'. This, again, requires an investment of time as we plan out the concepts that will reach the top rung, in terms of challenge.

Probing

If we are not careful an atmosphere develops in our rooms where students know that whatever they offer will be accepted; that we will nod compliantly and move on when they share their answers. A more productive and resilient classroom environment can be achieved if we develop the conditions that thrive on probing. Here, we cultivate real thinking and challenge, establishing the parameters for what a quality verbal answer looks like.

Rather than accepting a student's first answer (which often may be superficial in its depth), we should seek to encourage them to rephrase or offer more to their answer, or perhaps we 'bounce' a response around the room to encourage other assessments of the answer. We offer encouragement, but not finality; there is always more that can be added to points. Even if the probe is simply to expand the language that the student has employed, broadening and developing a rich vocabulary classroom will benefit students immeasurably. This will be evident when it comes to their ability to translate dialogue into effective outputs.

We want to build up an atmosphere of enquiry, where students have the confidence to challenge their own and other's thinking. If we can successfully model the probing phase with a class, eventually this will filter down to how students respond to each other. The pugnacious probe – one that seeks to accept only the best responses – will soon become the classroom norm.

Probing Phrases

1. 'That's a good start, how could we build on this further?'

2. 'What elements of that answer might we develop?'

3. 'Why do you think that is?'

4. 'Do we agree or disagree with this point?'

5. 'Could we disagree with or challenge that assumption?'

6. 'Can you say more?'

7. 'Can you explain that further?'

8. 'Why might we agree or disagree with that statement?'

These phrases can become much more lighthearted and competitive as we develop a relationship with a class; over time, they can be simply reduced to 'more', or 'why', or 'evidence'. Playing the devil's advocate can also be useful in taking the stress out of this situation for students, as we probe them into exhaustion; it lets them know that we are fulfilling a role to illicit better responses from them.

Differentiation

In our desire to differentiate our lesson content for varying abilities appropriately we often forget the easiest and slowest strategy – differentiation through questioning. It is simple: we consider carefully who we will select, using a hands-down approach, to answer a particular question. The way we phrase our questions will need to be skilfully adapted for the range of students we teach. As Martin Robertson suggests, 'The teacher should be in charge of who's going to make a contribution. Part of what you're trying to do is find out what they know and don't know' (Hendrick and Macpherson, 2017).

Hinge Questions

Hinge questions can provide a vital moment in a lesson and are one of the more effective assessment for learning strategies. Ultimately, they involve pausing the lesson at a 'hinge' point to provide students with a series of options on a topic. Often, they can function as multiple choice questions with one correct answer, and which ask students to justify their response. While this needs planning in advance, it is an excellent way to decide on the direction of a lesson. It allows teachers to check how well the class are progressing and address any misconceptions immediately. If a topic needs to be revisited to ensure understanding, this can then be immediately implemented.

Tackling the 'I Don't Know' Response

The curse of all responses to questioning is the glazed frown and 'I don't know' (or, in reality, 'dunno'). Often, this inspires a speedy leap to another student to provide the answer we are looking for. Tackling the 'I don't know' response is, however, important in reiterating a climate of high expectations in the classroom and motivating students. Doug Lemov's (2010) 'No Opt Out' strategy is a good starting point. This is where you ask another student the question, then return to the first student to ask them to explain how the answer has been arrived at. Alternatives are rephrasing the question, providing the answer and asking the student to explain it, or providing two contrasting answers and asking the student to explain which answer they feel is correct. Finally, we may give our students some time to come up with an answer in writing, giving them confidence before we ask for an answer. Either way, the 'I don't know' response should not escape our high expectations.

The same is true of classes that may well know how to answer, but who are quiet and reluctant to share their thinking. While the strategies in this chapter can assist in creating an ethos where they are more comfortable to share, there are pedagogical tricks that can help. Using mini whiteboards and asking them to hold up their answers to questions will remove some of the fear factor, as will providing students with numbers and asking them to answer if their number is called. Movement can also be helpful in encouraging more dialogue; asking students to go to different points in the room that represent a different can help to encourage them to justify their answers. A later chapter will look at how to support our more introverted students in more detail.

It would not be an exaggeration to suggest that all of the strategies above have at their core one common element in order to be done successfully: the capacity to build good relationships. The classroom is a deeply interpersonal environment, and learning effectively requires some degree of emotional connection. Deconstructing what can help us to build and develop these positive relationships in the next two chapters can help us to transform the lives of young people.

Slow Questions

1. Are you falling into the 'rapid-riffle approach' to questioning?

2. What other questioning traps do you need to be conscious of in your teaching?

3. What 'wait time' strategies could you easily implement into your teaching?

4. Are you getting the balance right between closed and open questioning?

5. Could you make more use of questioning as a form of differentiation in your lessons?

6. How could you script your questions for impact?

7. What strategies can you use to tackle the 'don't know' or quiet classes?

CHAPTER 7: TO PRAISE OR NOT TO PRAISE?

We've come a long long way together
Through the hard times and the good
I have to celebrate you baby
I have to praise you like I should.
'Praise You'

Fat Boy Slim

As teachers we have an intrinsic desire to build confidence, to nurture and to encourage. One of the idealistic reasons we entered the profession was to motivate the students who grace our classrooms and inspire them to achieve greater things. We work relentlessly to encourage students to feel a sense of pride, effort and commitment to our subjects.

From the very start of our teaching careers, we learn the importance of positivity in facilitating this motivation and maximising effort. And so, we praise. But, often, we don't stop: we offer praise too quickly, too repetitively – ultimately with little reflection. We utter 'excellent', 'outstanding', 'superb' and other such superlatives frequently in lessons, directing them towards the quality of work, responses and behaviour of our students. The reality is that in employing our praise so liberally, we influence the dynamic of a classroom profoundly, and not in the way that we perhaps envision or hope.

Over-Praising

As an NQT I suffered from a tragic case of effusive over-praising. I wanted students to try hard; I wanted them to see that I cared about their efforts. So, I resorted to what seemed like an easy win: praise, praise and more praise. Superlatives were tossed around like cheap confetti, exclaimed in response to even the most incoherent of grunted answers. My students' workbooks would be scrawled with more hyperbole – 'I absolutely love this' was a particular favourite. Then one noisy, rainy Monday afternoon the bleak reality struck: my praise obsession was actually making my students lazy and unresponsive.

It was on this day that my arch NQT nemesis (we all had one!) decided to inform me about the reality of my condition. Rolling her eyes with impeccable talent, she looked at me scathingly and said 'Is anything not excellent?'

While I admit that this student intimidated and terrified me on a number of levels, she really had me there. How do you counter that? Other than letting the ground metaphorically swallow me up, I decided there and then that I would no longer be so thoughtless with my praise. Daniel Willingham (2005) provides an apt summary of where I was going wrong:

> To motivate students – especially older students who are more discerning and better able to appreciate the differences between what is said and what is meant – teachers need to avoid praise that is not truthful, is designed to control behaviour, or has not been earned.

The first step in countering this is to consider how it feels to be the recipient of such praise.

Receiving Elevated Praise

First, a moment to consider the use of 'outstanding', for so long a benchmark for excellence in the educational world. When we define something as 'outstanding' the implication is there is no improvement needed; it is as good as it gets. To receive such feedback as adults would leave us glowing and, arguably, it would also convince us that there is nothing that we could do to improve further. This is very often not the case. In theory, nothing is 'outstanding'; everything has the capacity to be refined, improved and developed.

By using such terms so loosely, we perplex students by praising them for work that is not, perhaps, representative of real effort. Both we and they know it does not merit praise – it needs more work, care and attention to detail. Yet, often, we are hesitant to offer constructive feedback to young people, concerned about the impact that criticism will have on our relationship with that student.

The reality is that with lower-attaining students we often become more liberal with our use of praise. As Deborah Stipek (2010) argues, praise that seeks to nurture these students is actually serving to illustrate low expectations of what they are capable of achieving:

Praise for successful performance on an easy task can be interpreted by a student as evidence that the teacher has a low perception of his or her ability. As a consequence, it can actually lower rather than enhance self-confidence. Criticism following poor performance can, under some circumstances, be interpreted as an indication of the teacher's high perception of the student's ability.

Ultimately, it is high expectations and the refusal to accept anything but the best that will engender real motivation for all of our students. The high jump provides an interesting praise analogy: the higher we set the bar, the more our students will push themselves to leap clear of it. It is also important not to underestimate how robust our students are; they can take criticism and will strive to improve the quality of their work.

Dependency

Praising too often and too frequently generates a culture of dependency; it results in young people working only to be praised, rather than working to harness their own development and self-efficacy. All of us will be at the receiving end of feedback throughout our adult life, most of it in varying degrees of quality. Part of the purpose of education should be to familiarise young people with more honest and constructive feedback. We want to do our bit in developing adults who are comfortable using feedback to improve, not desperately seeking praise to make us feel good about ourselves and our work.

Specific Praise

We know that high-quality feedback is vital to learning and clarity in the classroom. In fact, John Hattie (2011) argues that it is one of the most significant factors in impacting on achievement. He summarises Sadler's research on the gap (1989) 'feedback is powerful when it reduces the gap between where the student is and where he or she is 'meant to be''. In order to maximise this feedback, students need to be aware of the goals they are working towards, and have a clear sense of what they are trying to achieve.

Hattie and Helen Timperley (2007) have also highlighted that 'Praise usually contains little task-related information and is rarely converted into more engagement, commitment to learning goals, enhanced self-efficacy, or understanding about the task.' In order to counter this, praise needs to move from the generic 'good' to providing specific feedback against learning goals. Judiciously employed, it can signal to students that they are going in the right direction with the task, and define clearly what skills they need to replicate as they continue working.

When praise is specific, it has the added value of helping our students to become more reflective about their learning. They will begin to recognise that if they mirror this precise positive feedback later, they will improve the quality of their work. Daniel Goleman (1996) writes that this further clarifies the importance of providing credible praise, stating that 'specificity is just as important for praise as for criticism. I won't say that vague praise has no effect at all, but it doesn't have much, and you can't learn from it.'

The value of specific praise and feedback is also mirrored in marking. Writing 'good' in the margin of a student's workbook is praise that is fairly meaningless, signalling nothing of any real use for students to move forward with their learning. It needs to be expanded on so that there is engagement from the student as to why this work is successful. This does not necessarily have to add to the teachers' workload; students can annotate their own work in response to feedback and try to identify why something has been identified as 'good'. This serves to develop their capacity for reflection and understanding about why something is effective. All we need to do is check their work and have follow up conversations with the student if there are misconceptions.

Linking the praise to the objective of the lesson – one of Doug Lemov's *Teach Like a Champion* (2010) techniques – is also very useful for maintaining a sense of direction and clarity. It helps in ensuring there is a consistency and a drive to the lesson, so that students know exactly what you want them to achieve. As Lemov (2015) notes, 'praising (or positively reinforcing) actions means calling out things like hard work and diligence, but some of the best teachers I've observed align their praise to learning objectives'. He goes on to highlight how this gives the room a real palpable sense of clarity about the desired outcomes as the lesson progresses.

Phrases

'You are going in the right direction in this task, because...'

'Well done, you are starting to achieve one of our objectives for this lesson...'

'You have completed that task well because...'

'This is a strong answer, because you have used...'

'I am impressed with your use of...'

Praising for Effort

Carol Dweck's (2012) research on mindsets has been hugely illuminating in highlighting that excessive praise can have self-defeating consequences. She argues that there are two very distinct mindsets. The first is the belief that intelligence is fixed. Dweck notes that 'Believing that your qualities are carved in stone – the fixed mindset – creates an urgency to prove yourself over and over'. This leads to a fear of risk-taking and an avoidance of anything that does not validate the opinion that our intelligence can be developed.

The converse of this – the 'growth mindset' – is clearly what we want to hone and encourage in young people; the belief that our intellectual ability can be developed over time. The implications for perseverance and learning are clear, as Dweck (2012) points out: 'You can see how the belief that cherished qualities can be developed creates a passion for learning. Why waste time proving over and over how great you are, when you could be getting better?'

When we praise a student for their intellectual ability – saying something like 'you are so clever' – we may have an instant positive impact. However, in doing this, we also reinforce the belief that their ability to complete tasks is correlated with their intellectual prowess. The moment they find themselves struggling to complete a task, their emotional resilience may not be as developed as a student with a growth mindset.

The nuances of how we use praise and encouragement in our classroom can help our students to develop the more favourable growth mindset. As far as possible, praise should be about process and effort rather than what might be perceived as ability. My naive NQT self was actually demotivating students quite drastically, making them at the most ambivalent about striving to achieve their best, but certainly unclear about what they could potentially achieve. Instead, praise for process and effort involves validating engagement, improvement, resilience and perseverance. We acknowledge and celebrate the students who have demonstrated real graft and resilience in seeking to overcome difficulty, regardless of their intellectual starting point.

Seeking ways to celebrate this culture of excellence and hard work are vital in inspiring a growth mindset. As Dweck (2016) has acknowledged, telling young people they can achieve anything will not work in isolation:

> Another misunderstanding [of growth mindset] that might apply to lower-achieving children is the oversimplification of growth mindset into just [being about] effort. Teachers were just praising effort that was not effective, saying "Wow, you tried really hard!".

Instead, effective praise needs to become part of a school's culture, to permeate every aspect of the ethos. As explored in the minimalistic environment chapter, the visual stimulus can encourage students to endeavour for excellence by showcasing excellent examples of student work. Shaun Allison and Andy Tharby (2015) highlight a case study of Les Quennevais School in Jersey, where the school has generated an 'Ethic of Excellence Wall'. This visually marks out quality work to students, encouraging them to strive to match those standards. The school argues that 'A big part of having a growth mind set is being inspired by the greatness of others'.

Phrases

'You have tried very hard with that task and achieved...'

'I like how carefully you have worked on that...'

'You have been very thoughtful and determined...'

'You have really persevered with that task, well done...'

'Mistakes are important, let's explore how that happened...'

Behavioural Praise

The management of attitudes and learning in our classrooms is a hugely complex area that we will explore in more detail in later chapters. One aspect of ensuring calm and consistent classrooms is how we moderate our language to reinforce positive behaviours. Praise for good behaviour is hugely illuminating and useful in the classroom, preventing us from delivering the constant diatribe of negativity that can dominate our language with more challenging groups. It models to young people the expectations you have of them and celebrates a positive classroom culture.

Spotting what is going right, rather than going wrong, and praising it clearly defines the behaviours that we want to see more from the whole class. It is one of the central philosophies in Chip and Dan Heath's book *Switch* (2011), in which the authors argue that finding 'bright spots' in any organisation can lead in creating change. As they note, 'These flashes of success – these bright spots – can illuminate the road map for action and spark the hope that change is possible'.

Praising our behaviour 'bright spots' in the classroom needs to be based on high expectations – it is not about merely praising students for taking a pen out. Instead, it involves setting the bar very high, then recognising when students are striving to achieve these levels of excellence. Drawing attention to this will hopefully see other students become keen to mirror the same positive behaviours.

Phrases

'Excellent focus and listening skills from you...'

'You have all worked beautifully in silence for that task...'

'Well done for a focused conversation on your work...'

'You entered the room calmly and started on the task straight away, well done...'

'All eyes are on me and you are ready to listen, excellent...'

Differentiated Praise

People can respond to praise in markedly different ways, and clearly interpersonal skills, sensitivity and empathy are vital when considering how to praise students meaningfully. There is certainly no one-size-fits-all mechanism for praising young people. We all know students who would curl up into a ball of embarrassment if they were publicly acknowledged and praised. These are the students who need quiet and focused moments of sincere praise to motivate and encourage them. Our ability to know the individuals who share our classrooms will help us to make informed choices about how best to motivate and encourage them.

Unexpected Praise

Predictability is the curse of any classroom. Effective praise also needs to be spontaneous and earned, not handed out predictably at the end of all the responses offered. Using praise when students least expect it, or being effusive about something they have done, will result in a smile and increased effort. Often, this can take the form of a postcard or note to the student, highlighting something that they have accomplished. Younger classes particularly enjoy this; it is a delight to watch their surprised faces light up.

Parental Engagement

Some of the most challenging students I have taught have been won over by taking time out of the busy day to engage with their parents. This may be through a brief phone call to highlight why their child has been chosen as 'Student of the Week' or 'Effort champion' for that particular week. Depending on the student, this information may be shared with the class, encouraging others to seek to attain these lofty heights. Parents are usually hugely grateful for this insight into their child's experience at school, particularly when the feedback they may frequently be on the receiving end of is less than positive.

Noticing

In *High Challenge, Low Threat* (2016a), Mary Myatt explores the power of noticing. She writes that 'to notice is to observe without preconceived ideas or judgements'. We are all complex individuals who want to be taken seriously for our endeavours. Praise in schools should not just be about our students; it should also be about validating the challenging work we teachers do as professionals. Stepping outside of our rooms and noticing the brilliant things our colleagues are doing, and meaningfully praising these efforts, helps to make both us and the people we work alongside feel good about our profession.

All the conflicting advice regarding the effective use of praise can lead to Hamlet-style levels of angst: 'to praise or not to praise, that is the question'. Hamlet himself, however, can provide us with solace. It is indeed 'nobler in the mind' to praise; but it is also an area in which the 'soft you now' approach works best. To hold back, link praise to learning goals and focus on effort might just motivate our students to achieve their best.

Slow Questions

1. Are you falling into over-praising with any of your students or groups?

2. What phrases could you adapt to make your praise more specific?

3. Is their scope in your classroom to make praise more related to effort?

4. Are you striving to encourage a 'growth mindset' in your classroom?

5. Are you looking for classroom 'bright spots' and praising students who demonstrate behaviour expectations?

6. How often are you positively engaging with parents?

7. Do you celebrate the commitment and support of the teachers who work alongside you?

PART III:
SLOW RELATIONSHIPS

CHAPTER 8:
REFINING RELATIONSHIPS

The most important single ingredient in the formula of success is knowing how to get along with people.
Theodore Roosevelt

What makes teaching worthwhile? What makes us crawl out of bed, at some ungodly time, on those cold, wet and miserable winter mornings? Of course, the answer to this is unique and personal to us all. Most teachers, however, would give significant credit to the professional satisfaction that working with young people can provide. That moment in which we share success with those who have graced our classrooms for weeks, months or even years, goes some way in validating the hours of work. The pleasure we get in the boundless variety and unique spark that young people offer, is one reason why we are committed to the teaching profession.

While we all find the way that is most natural to us to form these relationships, without them teaching can be a lonely and challenging world. As Ian Gilbert (2012) suggests:

> ...the one thing I learned from my teacher training is that teaching is about relationships. Once you get those right, children will leap through hoops of flame for you. Get them wrong – and it can feel like the other way round.

The Data Files

Most professions find themselves in a constant state of flux. Teaching, however, is refreshingly simple and for the most part, steady. We could return to a classroom from a hundred years ago and still be able to teach. One clear change, however, that separates us from our Victorian counterparts, is the increasingly important role data has started to play.

While the use of data to track students' progress has been transformational in raising modern standards in education, there is always the danger that the soul of teaching can become lost and replaced with something more mechanical. Arguably, some of the aspects of value-added, performance-related pay and the labels that are defining young people, can begin to challenge how much we prioritise honing the interpersonal aspects of teaching that have remained vital for generations.

Such labels negate the sensitivity and delicacy that is required to work effectively with young people; of which every single one presents something unique and different. If ever a profession fails when it is reduced to spreadsheets and tracking, it is in the teaching profession. As an interpersonal process, teaching is hugely complex, with its success partly founded on our capacity to use our awareness, intuition, communication skills and ability to empathise.

Beyond the Data

What makes a good teacher? As reflective practitioners we wrestle endlessly with this question and the extent to which we have reached our own high self-imposed standards. Yet, it is our customers – the students – who provide the most startlingly honest insights into this age-old question (and not many of them refer to any capacity to deconstruct data in their criteria!) Much of what has been explored already in this book will feature in their responses: subject knowledge, clarity and enthusiasm all rank highly. Unsurprisingly, it is the capacity to form positive relationships that is always central in feedback, the ability to connect with them and respect who they are as individuals.

How many students comment favourably on a teacher who always appeared to have time for them, meaning that their passion and success in that subject was cultivated? We all want to be acknowledged and to be recognised; if we are not, we start to become disillusioned and begin to lose any real sense of motivation. The same is true of the microcosm of the classroom; for young people, there is nothing worse than feeling invisible. There is also the fact that they spend hours in our company – they need to feel some sort of connection with us in order to help them learn effectively and feel comfortable with sharing ideas.

We need information and data – these are important to informing the decisions we make and how we plan for the success of our students. Yet, in the muddle of all this information tussling inside our tired and frantic teacher heads, the individual and their experience is often lost. We forget to pause and recognise who is sitting before us: a group of thirty young adults, each also wrestling with their own life outside the classroom. Remembering this will help us to begin to forge rapport and connections with our students, and help them to achieve their best.

Boundaries

It is both healthy and important that there are some parameters and boundaries in the relationship between a teacher and a student. There is a reason why professional detachment is necessary: we are here to educate children and to get the best out of them, not to be their friends. It is not about platitudes or being overly friendly; it is something more complex, nuanced and skilled that is required. The resounding quality must be *respect*: a relationship based on both warmth and professionalism. The following aspects are all part of this complex cocktail, beginning with the very human quality of empathy.

Teenage Kicks

What is life like for the modern teenager? How far is it from our own experience of adolescence? The most obvious difference is that social media and the impact of mobile phones on teenagers is seen everywhere; communication is instant and there is no escape from the incessant notifications. Dan Tapscott (2009) summarises young people's familiarity with technology in Grown Up Digital, stating that 'to this generation, the internet is like the fridge. They don't know the nuts and bolts of its operation; it's just a part of life'.

As a consequence, teenagers' lives are demonstrably more public than ever before, bringing with it a pressure to behave in ways that, as adults, most of us have no real conception of. Their lives are also louder: noise, conversation and activity filters through all aspects of daily experiences. This is clearly demonstrated when we face the uphill battle to train young people to work in silence; it is certainly not a behaviour that feels natural to a great number of them. It also means that concentration is more challenging for us to harness, and the slow values that are vital – listening skills, attention, focus and perseverance – are all the more important to actively model and teach.

This is combined with the reality about what we are encouraging young people to do: thinking is challenging and represents everything that today's instant society is not. As Daniel Willingham (2010) argues 'Compared with your ability to see and move, thinking is slow, effortful, and uncertain'. Young people are also going through a complex maturing process. Their brains are in a state of flux, with their pre-frontal cortex not yet fully formed, meaning that they have a reduced capacity to manage emotions and make decisions.

The challenges that students face – fluctuating emotions, incessant communication and problems with thinking – are generally not high on teachers' daily agenda. They are, of course, only a snapshot of the range of other complex factors that may influence how young people feel. Our main purpose is to teach – we are not surrogate therapists or, indeed, surrogate parents. Yet, in order to teach, we need to have some conception of the daily experience of young people. This empathy is a vital component of any effective practitioner in the classroom. Daniel Goleman (1996) notes that without empathy a person is 'emotionally tone deaf', which is a disaster for anyone in a profession where interpersonal skills play such a vital role.

Intellectual development and emotional development are very much correlated. It is vital to pause and look at things from different perspectives. This sense of understanding will allow us to be more patient, more understanding and better able to get the best out of our students.

Individuality

Half way through my second year of teaching, I took over a class from a very experienced teacher following a timetable change. In preparation for the changeover, this wonderful teacher handed me what could only be described as a dossier of information about the class. Each student had a page of handwritten information about them, documenting their strengths and their weaknesses in English and a dissection of their characters. What this powerfully demonstrated to me was just how well that teacher knew each individual student, and how much she valued their continued development in her subject. It is a moment that has resonated with me since, and has become a yardstick I use to measure how well I know the students I teach. Can I speak at length about their strengths, weaknesses and who they are as a person in my class?

Inevitably, achieving this requires the capacity to step off the continuous teacher treadmill of activity and make time to discover information about the young people we teach. It is about finding out what motivates and interests them. Be it a sport, a hobby or a particular book that they are reading, students treasure the interactions where we take a genuine interest in their experiences outside of the classroom. It is all about the power of connections, something that can be achieved through the simple routine of greeting students by name as they enter the classroom. Mary Myatt (2016a) expands on the merits of this in *High Challenge, Low Threat*, arguing that:

> Teachers do this when they are waiting for their students to arrive. Whether they are standing at the door as they come in to the lesson, or

are already inside, they convey a warmth which says I am glad you are here, I'm glad that you are in my lesson, we are going to be doing some interesting things today.

As we have seen, having positive body language and facial expressions when we interact with young people is vital. Remembering to smile and engage on a personal level will help in forging a stronger relationship with students. With a class who we might view as more challenging, this process becomes even more important. It sends subliminal messages that we are clam, positive and in control.

From the moment students enter the classroom, our enthusiasm is also a defining factor in how they will respond to us. Enthusiasm stems from the Greek word 'enthousiazein' which translates as to be inspired by the 'the god within' – a delightful way to consider our inner fire and how that 'god within' can motivate our students. Passion and positively are, as we know, hugely infectious. We need to resonate with the message that we enjoy teaching all of our classes. By giving this impression we are much more likely to create a positive learning experience for both us and our students.

Listening

Perhaps one of the most underrated teacher qualities is the ability to genuinely listen. In fact, given the nature of the profession, often we are more predisposed to talk than we are to listen. Given this tendency, when we do listen, we often forget to understand what a student is saying, and seek only to consider our own reflections on how we could offer a suitable response.

However, we form real connections with people when we show that we are both genuinely interested, and have time to listen to what they have to offer. It is the most useful way to develop an understanding of an individual and see the reality of how they are feeling. The near-absence of quality listeners in the school environment means that it is all the more wonderful when a student discovers someone who will invest time in listening to how they really feel. As Marcus Aurelius (2004) wisely stated, 'practice really hearing what people say. Do your best to get inside their minds'.

Role Modelling

There is no denying that we are under the microscope in our role as teachers. Students watch us carefully, and demonstrating consistent behaviour is one of the ways we can ensure they develop both confidence and faith in us. It involves role modelling the skills they may not see elsewhere: clarity, calmness, warmth and direction. Providing a sense of consistency, an emotionally safe environment that they can feel nurtured in, must be one of the defining aims in our classrooms.

This is manifested most obviously in our interactions – when we meaningfully use eye contact; when we are polite and warm in our tone; when we show compassion – in all these instances, we are building up a sense of trust with that student.

Our Characters

There needs to be something more that young people can connect with, rather than just a body – a teacher façade – at the front of the room who they spend an hour a day with. There is a fine line here, a delicate balance between over-sharing and too much frankness with students; however, they do need to gain some sense of us as individuals. While that might not be sharing our most intimate secrets and hobbies, it is about dropping in aspects of our personalities, or even tantalising hints about our wildly exciting lives beyond the classroom.

It is important that we are authentic and at ease in our different approaches. In our drive to power through the curriculum, and in a data-infused blindness, we can often forget the value that a touch of humour can have in turning a lesson on its head.

The objective is not to be a stand-up comedian but it is, perhaps, about not taking ourselves too seriously and not shying away from making jokes at our own expense. Teachers at the beginning of their careers are often too nervous to present this version of themselves; yet, it serves to break down barriers and improve relationships. A teacher I once observed was a spectacular user of puns. While the students groaned in mock disgust when she launched into another pun from her repertoire, in reality you could see the delight in their eyes. Pausing to inject some humour serves to relax our students, to refocus them and to energise the room.

The Introvert/Extrovert divide

Despite our best efforts, there are always students in our classrooms who are dominated by their more boisterous and extroverted peers. They are the victims of utterly trite and superfluous feedback on reports and during parents' evenings: 'lovely and hardworking but should try to contribute more'. In the busy maze of the school day, it becomes challenging to find the time to nurture and empower these students.

Susan Cain's Quiet (2013) is a vital read for those seeking to improve their ability to empathise with those quieter and more reflective souls. As Cain acknowledges, 'The truth is that many schools are designed for extroverts'. We can, however, improve our awareness of this and take positive steps to bring out the best in the more introverted students. Cain continues by saying, 'don't forgot to cultivate the shy, the gentle, the autonomous, the ones with single-minded enthusiasms for chemistry sets or parrot taxonomy or nineteenth-century art. They are the artists, engineers, and thinkers of tomorrow'.

The first important step is in valuing and celebrating the diversity and individuality in our classrooms, understanding that to be quiet is something to be cherished, not belittled. It is then about seeking to make the conditions suitable to allow our quieter students to flourish. This might require more thinking time to allow them to formulate their thoughts, or it might be about structuring any group work sensitively.

While every young person is different, the mechanism for praising and building a positive relationship with a more reticent student might also differ. The best approach might be a quiet word on an individual basis or a postcard that captures something in writing. Most importantly, when communicating with parents, avoiding criticism for participation levels and seeking to celebrate the other diverse qualities that quieter students possess can let them know they are both accepted and valued.

Outside the Classroom

The dynamic of a classroom can often hamper attempts to build genuine relationships, with students and teachers instantly morphing into their assumed roles. A school, however, is so much more than just its individual classrooms, and it is outside of the classroom walls that we can appear most human. Using duty times or the time when we are out in the corridors to facilitate conversations with students will help. Slowing down and engaging with the young people who surround us, and enquiring about them, helps us to generate connections that will improve relationships. While it may at first seem to be yet another time stealer, in reality it is, as Ian Gilbert (2012) notes, 'an investment of your time and energy that pays back many times in many ways'.

Embracing the extracurricular life of a school can also transform relationships with individual groups. This could be running a sports team, or going on a school residential trip as a chaperone. One of my most rewarding experiences as a teacher was taking a group of Year 12 students to India to do some charity work. Such trips can give young people experiences and memories they will never forget.

The majority of students we encounter will be nothing but delightful: eager to learn, receptive and keen to forge positive relationships with us. Yet, it would be naïve to believe that teaching does not raise its own challenges in terms of student behaviour. In fact, the exhaustion and frustration caused by the management of poor behaviour is one of the main reasons why some teachers leave the profession early. Hopefully, the principles explored in this chapter will go some way in securing positive relationships with students based on trust, respect and learning. However, we also need to be prepared with strategies to manage more challenging students; it is time to equip ourselves with some behaviour armoury.

Slow Questions

1. Are you making enough time outside of your busy teaching day to prioritise building positive relationships?

2. Is the empathetic mindset present in your interactions with young people?

3. Are you communicating genuine enthusiasm (your god within!) in the presence of all your students?

4. How well are you listening to students both inside and outside of the classroom?

5. Are you conscious of the introvert/extrovert divide and using strategies to positively engage with both?

6. Could you involve yourself in more activities outside of the classroom to generate positive relationships with students?

CHAPTER 9:
SERENE AND STOICAL
BEHAVIOUR MANAGEMENT

We cannot choose our external circumstances, but we can always choose how we respond to them.
Epictetus

A short journey through the remarkable life of the philosopher Epictetus will demonstrate why his words open a chapter exploring the mystery of effective behaviour management. Born around 50 AD, he arrived in Rome without a family, as the property of the rich and powerful Epaphroditus. This lovely chap was particularly cruel to Epictetus, twisting his leg until it broke and leaving him lame. Epictetus was later set free from captivity, although any joy was short-lived as he was then banished from Rome by the ruthless Emperor Domiltian. Undeterred by his evident lack of good fortune, he went on to form a popular stoical school of thought within philosophy.

One of the central principles of his philosophy is the capacity to remain calm in the face of adversity and control one's emotions, no matter what the provocation (qualities of character that, to this day, are referred to as 'being stoical'). As Alain de Botton (2001) has clarified, stoicism is not a 'recipe for passivity and quietude' but, rather, about our priorities and focusing on what we can control and influence. Epictetus (2008) himself provides an apt summary – 'It is not what happens to you, but how you react to it that matters'. Here we have the perfect starting point for a path to calm and consistent behaviour management in our schools.

Low-Level Disruption

There is no debating the importance of effective behaviour management in the classroom. Like everyone else, I am very aware of the utter frustration that comes from ruined teaching experiences due to poor behaviour. There is no quick fix, no speedy 'top ten strategies' to instantly employ which will guarantee compliance and 'outstanding behaviour'. In fact, many cases of escalating poor behaviour are the consequence of reacting too quickly to the emotional impulses of the heart, rather than the serene thinking of the mind. Instead, as Paul Dix (2017) argues, our own actions are vital:

> In behaviour management, culture eats strategy for breakfast. Getting the culture right is pivotal. With the right culture the strategies that are used become less important. The culture is set by the way that the adults behave.

One of the most important steps we can take in the organisation of our classrooms is to see behaviour management as, in part, a deeply interpersonal and emotional process. It is founded on our ability to manage not just our own emotions but also the fluctuating hormones of thirty adolescents. In order to secure calm and clarity in the classroom, we need to be aware of what Vincent van Gogh (1889) called 'the little emotions that are the great captains of our lives'.

Self-awareness

Despite our utopian fantasies, our students are not going to meekly comply with our every request . A small proportion of them are likely to want to do anything but listen, or act in the manner we are cajoling them into. This extract, from Haim G. Ginott's book *Teacher and child* (1972), defines how our own attitude has a profound influence on the young people we teach:

> I've come to a frightening conclusion that I am the decisive element in the classroom. It's my personal approach that creates the climate. It's my daily mood that makes the weather. As a teacher, I possess a tremendous power to make a child's life miserable or joyous. I can be a tool of torture or an instrument of inspiration. I can humiliate or heal. In all situations, it is my response that decides whether a crisis will be escalated or de-escalated and a child humanized or dehumanized.

While students will display behaviour that doesn't conform with our expectations, teachers should ideally radiate consistency, clarity and calmness. We are, after all, the adults in the room. Focusing instead on what we do have ownership of will help us to begin to manage behaviour proactively.

There are many things that we do have control over: ensuring that the content of the lesson is interesting and challenging; demonstrating real ownership of our classrooms; streamlining our communication with regards to behaviour and ensuring it is clear and assertive; being relentlessly consistent in our applications of rules and structures; making sure we are working hard to build positive and meaningful relationships. We do this while remembering that we are all part of a wider-school system that needs to be meticulously adhered to.

Systems

Maverick behaviour management that divorces itself from the rules of the school does not work. Attempting to do so isolates you in the eyes of students from the wider behaviour network that is consistently applied elsewhere. It also undermines colleagues who are working to secure excellent whole-school behaviour. It is our responsibility to use the structures and mechanisms put in place by the school that facilitate consistency. This is not about passing the responsibility for managing behaviour to someone else; it is about transparency.

Initially, this requires immediate familiarisation with the behaviour policies in the school. What sanction and reward systems are in place? From the first day with a new class, you must go about immediately implementing these policies, showing that you have extremely high expectations for the conduct of students in your classroom that match with the ethos and routines the school has in place.

Young people are savvy: they can immediately sense if there is a hesitancy, reluctance or, indeed, insecurity about our ability to implement whole-school systems. They will then ruthlessly exploit this hesitancy and, before long, it can be challenging to decide with whom and when to use sanctions – a sure-fire way for behaviour management to break down. The quicker we get the message across that disruption will not be tolerated in our classroom, the less it spreads. A meticulously thought-out seating plan also goes a long way towards highlighting expectations of control to students; one that can be adapted and changed when a more nuanced understanding of a class develops is most useful.

The same applies to the importance of knowing students' names and the diverse personalities they bring to our lessons as quickly as possible. Investing time in finding out about new students before they join our class can be hugely powerful in ensuring a seamless transition of positive behaviour.

One of the defining elements of any successful school is how robustly senior management are able to deal with poor behaviour. While we will look at the measured and strategic escalation for management of behaviour shortly, it is vital to remember that communication in a school must be honest and open from day one. Taking the time to discuss issues that may be developing in your class with colleagues and management is important, both in terms of sharing good practice and making sure poor behaviour is quickly addressed.

There is an element of competitive bravado about behaviour management. Admitting to having behavioural challenges is arguably something we are less likely to do, compared to asking for help with how best to teach or structure a lesson. Yet, it is an arbitrary distinction; behaviour management is just another aspect of teaching, and should be discussed as openly.

Rules and Routines

It is not primitive or gladiatorial to recognise that it is essential that we set rules and routines in order to ensure simplicity in our classrooms. This is one aspect of classroom culture in which didacticism does indeed reign supreme, and it is up to us as the adults in the room, to enforce what those rules and routines are. Tom Bennett writes that 'instead of leaving behavioural choices up to chance, the best strategy is for teachers to draw up exactly what is expected of their students from the beginning of their relationship' (Hendrick and Macpherson, 2017). The idea that students construct the rules of the classroom is not the most assertive and clear way in which to begin to illustrate how a classroom should function.

Often, gradually introducing students to some of the principles of the classroom is more effective. Beginning lesson one with a list of ten key rules tends to wash over young people's heads (particularly if it is period five at the start of a new term; they will have heard this message four times already). In the first lesson with a new group, what is more likely to encourage a positive attitude is our passion and enthusiasm. Begin by engaging them in the mystery of what they will learn about in our wonderful subjects.

In the first few lessons, visibly demonstrating the rules of the classroom when occasions arise is more likely to ensure transparency about what is expected. This is complemented by the sense of control you can evoke through having an organised and clear environment, with everything in place to ensure a well-ordered lesson. All of these approaches transmit both clear and subliminal messages about authority and control, much more powerfully than a list of classroom rules can do.

So, what are those values that we want to be crystal clear on with young people – the essentials of easeful and well-managed classroom functioning?

Essential: Sacred Silence

To secure real and genuine silence needs repetitive training. Initially, this is modelled through our own delivery. There cannot be any murmur of dissent while we speak at the front of the room. The moment that there is and we talk over our students, we are on a very rapid slope to an uncontrolled classroom. With challenging classes this might require a war of attrition at the start of the year: frequent stopping, sanctioning and reminders about why silence is important during individual tasks. As Bill Rogers (2007) notes:

> When teachers talk over residual noise (of students chattering, or looking out of windows, or loudly fiddling with pens, rulers, pencil cases or toys, or calling out to get teacher attention) it habituates that such behaviour is 'tolerated' or 'does not really matter.'

It is vital that *we* set the parameters for volume control in our lessons, not the students.

This requires real clarity about what silence is and why it is important that we work in it. I deem it 'sacred silence' and try to have at least ten minutes in every lesson where students work in silence. There is a temptation to set students off doing silent work, then speed into the midst of them, waving a red pen manically or speaking loudly to them and detracting from the peace we are seeking to secure. Pausing, standing at the front of the room and observing students for a period of time after asking them to work independently is a good way to ensure their focus. They realise they are being observed and are more likely to get settled into independent work.

Essential: All eyes on me and pens down

Any well-ordered classroom has this philosophy at its heart. Attentiveness and listening is impossible if a young person is waving a pen around like a Potter wand, or if they are peering around seeking to engage the attention of a chum. Once this has been coached effectively at the start of the year, 'all eyes on me' needs frequent reminders and repetitive guidance. As the year goes on, both teachers and students become lax at enforcing this. The best behaviour gurus are those who are bordering on obsessive in ensuring consistency with this key message.

Here, the pause comes into confident force; waiting at the front of the room until we have all young people facing our way. Doug Lemov's (2015) SLANT technique is particularly helpful, ingraining successful learning habits:

S – sit up

L – listen

A – ask and answer questions

N – nod your head

T – track the speaker.

Essential: Respect

There is a fundamental misunderstanding in the autocratic approach to behaviour management, in which we seek to intimidate and scare young people into submission. While this may breed fear and compliance from some students, it will not engender genuine respect or, indeed, the conditions that will best enable learning. Instead, it is important that respect becomes the automatic behaviour in a classroom. This happens not by magic, but through real effort to remind and model to students the manner in which to behave.

Too often in the modern school environment we are not firm enough with low-level behaviour that is dismissive of us as teachers. The minute we let a student answer back rudely or roll their eyes at us, we send a significant message to the rest of the class: in this classroom it is acceptable to display openly disrespectful behaviours. If we want respect to filter through all aspects of our classroom we need to have the bar set high. That means that we need to carefully model such behaviour, making 'please' and 'thank you' the accompanying tools to all instructions and conversations in this mission. By lacing even the most obvious of imperatives with a 'thank you', we add to the atmosphere in the classroom. Coupling all this with a smile and a professional attitude will help us to develop relationships. Tom Sherrington (2017) argues that 'great teachers foster relationships with their students based on mutual respect, where there are no arguments about the expected standards of behaviour'.

Essential: Assertiveness

One of the fundamental challenges of entering the teaching profession is the requirement to immediately adapt how we communicate with groups of people. Never before have we had to employ such a plethora of tones and pitches, and act in mock fury if things are not completed to the standard we expect. Often, we have come directly from institutions in which our intellect, not our capacity to sustain order, is what has been valued.

Yet, if we are not assertive in our classrooms, if we are meek and indecisive, then learning will not flourish, but poor behaviour will. The most basic expectation we need to have is the presumption that young people will immediately follow our instructions. If they make the active choice not to follow them, we need to reveal utter incredulity, then we need to sanction appropriately.

Assertiveness is assisted when we detach the behavioural feedback we give from the child to the behaviour itself. We highlight what the student is doing wrong in terms of their actions, avoiding commenting on them as an individual. It is clear, concise and calm; for example, 'That behaviour you are demonstrating is not what we expect in this classroom.'

Essential: Eye Contact

Assertiveness and eye contact go hand in hand. Coupling an imperative with a prolonged piece of eye contact goes some way in ensuring that a young person complies with a request. The deadly stare is one that some teachers appear to have been born with, but others can easily practise and replicate. Slowly shaking the head in disbelief and a glare can be enough to result in some students whimpering in submission and returning to focus on their work. As stated earlier, the way we distribute eye contact around the room is also important in ensuring focus and positive behaviours from our students. Managing to hone the 'eyes on the back of their head' reputation among students is a clear sign of behaviour guru status!

The sense of control and composure that eye contact can give us is also reaffirmed by the body language points from Chapter 4. Doug Lemov (2015) suggests how the pace in which we approach an issue can subliminally highlight control:

> Walk slowly as you approach a situation where you have to intervene in behaviour. This can give you a few precious seconds to compose yourself and choose your words carefully. It also signals to students that you are calm and composed.

Essential: Positivity

When we react quickly and emotionally, we tend to reiterate the negatives. We can bombard the more difficult classes with a tirade of negativity about their inability to behave as we wish. We then enter a self-perpetrating cycle: our frequent pessimism spurs on the class to resent us and respond, in turn, with more similar behaviours.

Despite what may feel like the encroaching darkness of a difficult class, there will be 'superstars' nestled in the corner, who do everything we ask of them. As explored in Chapter 7 when we discussed giving praise, taking the time to identify the correct behaviour young people are demonstrating will hopefully give those students who may be caught in bravado the opportunity to self-regulate their actions through mirroring their classmates' behaviour.

Most young people want to please their teachers; some just need more guidance on exactly how to do it. The more vocal and celebratory we are about positive behavioural patterns, the more they will diffuse throughout the classroom. As another stoic, Marcus Aurelius (2008), would have it: 'Dwell on the beauty of life. Watch the stars and you will see yourself running'.

Essential: Escalation

Any successful behaviour management system should be founded on a slow and progressive series of warnings and sanctions. There needs to be complete clarity about what the process is for escalating poor behaviour. Once we are confident in exactly what the system is, it reduces effective behaviour management to a consistent ladder-style approach.

While consistency is vital, subtlety and interpersonal skill are also essential. Some of our less lovable students may deliberately seek to engage us in very public confrontations that can hijack learning. Students watch us like hawks and revel in attention. Using words quietly and on a private, individual level rather than publicly berating them will help to maintain the atmosphere of calm. In the face of repeated disruption, it is about patiently going through the behavioural stages that make up a school policy. Students also have a ferocious need to diagnose anything they think may be the slightest deviation from their conception of fairness. It is important, therefore, that we are consistent and fair when distributing sanctions; nobody should be exempt.

Essential: Follow up

I have been very lucky to work under departmental heads who are utterly ruthless in their determination to ensure their departments are provided with the conditions that enable them to focus on teaching. One of the most obvious ways this is achieved is by not letting students feel they can get away with incidents of poor behaviour. Too often things can slip through the net: a detention is missed with a poor excuse, or incomplete homework is abandoned. The moment this is left unchallenged it sends immediate signals about the capacity of us as teachers, or as a whole school, to deal with bad behaviour.

The same goes with contacting parents. Most parents are hugely supportive of schools' desires to ensure their children succeed. These conversations, clearly, are vital. Again, refraining from commenting on the young person themselves, and outlining their positive qualities in your classroom, will help to ensure that we unite parents in our endeavour to achieve the best for their child.

The Role of Anger

Nobody wants to be in the company of a teacher whose only mode of communication comes from an almighty roar. In the face of repeated shouting, the damage to both relationships and learning in the classroom is significant. Yet, it would be naïve to believe that anger is not present when working with young people. We are only human and often invest time and energy into lessons that may be being repeatedly hijacked. The key is to use anger only in a manner that is measured and controlled, and never to expose ourselves as being too emotionally vulnerable in front of a class. When we feel ourselves growing in frustration and anger, this advice from Seneca (2003) is useful: 'The greatest remedy for anger is delay'. Seek to pause, gain perspective then apply the appropriate sanctions.

A display of anger or changing the tone of our voices works best when it is brief and followed by an immediate return to the calm that preceded it. On rare occasions, I may switch to an exaggerated glimpse of the raised Scottish voice, then return to passivity – all rather disconcerting! Some teachers, however, manage classes impeccably without ever having to raise their voices beyond a whisper. The trick is to find the persona that you feel most comfortable with and that works in maintaining the focus of students. Either way, students need to know that we are capable of anger and disappointment; it signposts, again, that we care about their success in the future. Paul Dix (2017) calls it 'deliberate botheredness'. We need to go out of our way to show young people that we care about them and their future.

Observations

Effective behaviour management is an art; one that, like any aspect of teaching, is always developing, maturing and improving throughout our careers. The key is to never become complacent and believe that we have mastered 'behaviour'. When I moved to a new school after a number of years of teaching, I was given a real eye opener with a challenging Year 9 class. The situation needed lots of careful reflection to prevent lessons going spectacularly amiss. There will never be a stage where we have learned all there is to learn about behaviour management; there is always a new, interesting and challenging group of youngsters waiting in the wings.

Finding behaviour role models, watching their lessons and studying how they make it appear utterly seamless has had the most impact in developing my own confidence in the classroom. It is then about mirroring some of those behaviours in a way that is natural. Trying to fight the behaviour battle in isolation can be utterly demoralising; opening up to the methods of other teachers leads to both solace and proactive solutions.

Perspective

That outrageously difficult class that seem to be specifically designed to test you to the very limit will make you a better teacher. They will foster in you a warrior-like attitude that refuses to be beaten; they will make you more assertive; they will ensure that you don't take your planning or your ability to hone relationships with young people for granted. As Seneca (2003) would again define it: 'difficulties strengthen the mind, as labour the body'.

One of the first groups I taught as an NQT in a comprehensive in central London was an all-boys Year 11 bottom set, consisting of around fifteen students. That was the quickest and most destructive learning curve I have been on. It was never perfect but, by the end of the year, I had survived, and some of the best moments of the school year were when things clicked with that group. In my second year, with a similar group, I was armed and ready not to repeat the same mistakes.

There will be lessons that fail and times when classes appear to wilfully ignore our every command. What we are in control of is our emotional response: not to bury our heads in the sand, not to capitulate in despair. Instead we must embrace the stoical approach, continue to learn and grow, and get planning for a much more positive experience in the next lesson.

Slow Questions

1. Do you focus on what you can proactively control when reflecting on behaviour?

2. Are you self-aware and able to moderate emotion when working with challenging classes?

3. Is there consistency and calm at the heart of your classroom persona?

4. Are you applying whole-school behaviour policies rigorously in your work in school?

5. Are the behaviour essentials imbedded in your work with each of your classes?

6. What other aspects of stoical philosophy could you apply to your teaching?

PART IV:
SLOW CLASSROOM
STRATEGIES

CHAPTER 10
THE POWER OF MODELLING

*Example is not the main thing in
influencing others. It is the only thing.*
Albert Schweitzer

'They just don't pay any attention.' 'Yet again, they haven't understood.' 'Why doesn't anyone listen anymore?' These teacher miseries can be heard in every staffroom across the country. Just how often do we berate students for what appears to be their glaring inability to translate lesson time into a quality final output in their workbooks? How often are we left tearing out what remains of our hair, as we slave away for hours marking work that has no resemblance to the glorious masterpieces we had envisioned?

The Blame Game

To place the blame on students for a poor final output is utterly wasted and misdirected energy. It negates our role as the organiser, facilitator and director of that final piece of work. It is tough to take at times, but the responsibility for a whole-class failure to understand how to approach a task lies solely with us. Instead, we need to reflect on how we might have approached our teaching of the task differently in order to improve the quality of the final piece of student work.

Let's examine the process that led to these poor final outcomes. Perhaps a variant of the following was used: we presented, deconstructed and discussed the task; we showed our students what we thought was a spectacular success criteria (or, even better, we constructed it together); we gave them (if useful for our subjects) a detailed plan or checklist; then, we set them off and relaxed in the corner, confident in our assumptions that students had the 'passport to success'.

In the race to get students started on their work, we have neglected what might be the essential final element in influencing their understanding: demonstrating both the thought process and what the final outcome of the task should look like. Modelling is beautiful in its slow simplicity; it is the process by which we make everything explicit for our students. We begin to close the gap between their understanding at that moment and where we want them to arrive at. In our planning stage, going through this thinking means we know exactly what the outcome is we are aiming to guide students towards and, thus, in our teaching it means the room for error is reduced.

The Value of Modelling

Design and technology was my Achilles heel in school and, if questioned, I am confident my wife would certainly not give a glowing testament to the quality of my DIY skills. (I fully embody all English teacher stereotypes.) My brother-in-law, on the other hand, happens to be a farmer and is extremely proficient in the DIY department.

In the process of writing this book we had a tiling emergency (middle-class dilemmas), which required me to quickly put up some new tiles in the bathroom. Cue the arrival of both a rather terrifying looking tile cutter and said brother-in-law to prevent any bloody disasters. Thirty minutes later and I, the most incompetent of DIYers, am slicing tiles to perfection.

Was this due to my brother-in-law's concise explanation of how to employ the tile cutter? Was it his 'five essential things to remember while tile cutting' list? (He is a man who takes DIY very seriously.) Was it my vacant and panicked nodding in response to his 'are you sure you have got this' line of questioning? Of course not! I gleaned how best to use it from the process of watching him complete the task, from his modelling of every stage of the tile cutting adventure.

The Research

Barak Rosenshine (2012) evaluated research to identify ten key principles for effective instruction (obviously my brother-in-law gave this a perusal before his tile-cutting instruction). The importance of modelling is his fourth principle: 'Students need cognitive support to help then to learn to solve problems. The teacher modelling and thinking aloud while demonstrating how to solve a problem are examples of effective cognitive support'. The distinction between novice and experts in the classroom is particularly important here: the expert guides the novice by illustrating exactly how they would approach the task themselves.

Peps Mccrea (2017) calls this additional cognitive support the 'faded transition experience between presentation and practice'. This helps to secure our students' understanding of exactly what it is we require them to do, avoiding any lack of clarity and the ambiguity that can fill our evenings with marking miseries.

The Assessment Criteria Conundrum

Often, the 'faded transition' that Mccrea highlights is absorbed by the analysis of assessment criteria. We cursively flick on a PowerPoint that reveals the five vital aspects of the assessment criteria and read them through with students. At times, we might offer them a 'student-friendly' interpretation of the criteria in an attempt to make it clearer for them. Yet, often the language is oblique and challenging to understand in isolation, particularly for adolescents trying to apply this to their work.

Then we set them off with the hope that the criteria will magically appear, despite them having no real conception of how it actually applies to their final piece of work. Daisy Christodoulou (2017) makes this clear, stating that 'As we've seen again and again, it's hard to define quality in prose, and prose descriptors can be interpreted in many different ways'. Replacing confusion-inspiring criteria with a model answer will help to facilitate clearer outcomes.

Reflective Modelling

As with any pedagogical tool, modelling has to be used thoughtfully, with the following three areas needing further reflection when planning their use in our lessons:

1. **Demotivating:** If we decide to share a student's, or our own work, with a class in the guise of it being a strong response, we need to make sure that it does not cripple confidence and result in demotivated students. Ideally, it should be of a standard that is challenging yet reachable for young people. Spending hours crafting a degree-level history essay on the Tudors is not likely to serve much purpose. Remembering our audience and the appropriate level is crucial to the effectiveness of a teacher-prepared model.

2. **The speed model:** For a model answer to be useful and productive in a classroom environment, there needs to be time invested in evaluating its strengths and weaknesses. Too often, I have been in lessons in which a model answer is flashed briefly up on a PowerPoint, where its qualities and nuances are utterly lost on the young people it has been designed to assist. Doing this serves only to intimidate, or indeed confuse students, as they haven't been given the scope to explore it in detail. As we will see, it is slowing this process down, unpicking and deconstructing a model response that will result in learning gains.

3. **Curtailing creativity:** As with all teaching strategies, the final aim is to encourage gradual ownership and more independence. After all, young people will not sit their exams with a delightfully constructed pre-answer nestled beside them. They will have to produce the work in the time available and with no scaffolds to assist them. There is an argument that using exemplary answers leads only to spoon-feeding, with our students copying these rather than using their initiative. While they say imitation is the sincerest form of flattery, we certainly don't produce answers in order for them to be copied. In this respect, careful and strategic thinking is required. We need to plan for moments when we see exactly how well our students can 'blindly' approach a task or a piece of work, in order to be sure about what they are capable of producing in an exam situation.

Using Teacher Exemplars

There is an insecurity that makes us hesitant to compose an exemplar answer for a class in advance. This is entirely understandable, as it demonstrates vulnerability, transparency and the risk of failure. The reality is, however, that these are qualities we try to inspire in our students every day; the qualities of reflective learners. By completing work for them, we show our students that we too are open to feedback, criticism and improvement. Alongside this is the obvious counter to intellectual insecurities: no matter how eloquent and radiating with intelligence our class may appear to be, they are not armed with an appropriate degree in a specialist area. Students want to know that they are in the hands of an expert, and when we produce something for them we signal that we are confident practitioners and know exactly what it is that we require of them.

The important thing is not to present them with a model in a dogmatic and arrogant fashion, waving around our 'masterpiece'; instead, the aim is to offer it as a tentative exploration of a question, if our subject allows it. In doing so we encourage students to see both the positives and the areas for development, reminding them that all work can be refined and improved (although, watch them take far too much glee in pointing out your inadequacies!)

The process of annotating a model answer is one that, ironically, will need to be modelled. Perhaps the first model answer could be provided pre-annotated, demonstrating strengths and areas for development. This can then function as a starting point in clarifying how work should be annotated in the future. It also requires slow and patient questioning, to check young people have understood exactly what approach has been taken in the model answer and can rationalise why that is effective.

In relation to dependence on the model, there are a number of tricks. Having a teacher answer to refer to in students' books is a powerful way to ensure the valued use of it as a resource; it can be used as a point of reference and for revision. Asking for exemplar to be returned every time can result in less learning gains. Instead, changing the question based on similar skills will prevent any direct copying.

As John Hattie (2013) notes, another way to work towards independence is to show a partially completed model answer. He writes that 'In many cases it is possible to show students fully worked examples, then to introduce exams that are only partially completed. This type of worked example is generally called a completion example'. Students will be then expected to go on to complete the work in the same style, using the modelled openings to support them.

Modelling Misconceptions

As influential as the slow expert approach to modelling is the reverse: presenting students with a poorly composed, rushed answer to a question. Instead of guiding them through a trajectory of quality, we use this as the opportunity to discuss the frequent stumbling blocks that may prevent them from completing the task well. By signposting the areas in which the students may go wrong, we help in building their awareness while they complete the task, increasing the likelihood of them producing effective answers.

Even better is to hold back the revelation that this is a poorly constructed piece of work and ask students to take on the role of the marker or examiner. At this point we ask for their initial thoughts on the work before pointing out the faults. If they have a good conception of how to structure a task, they should be able to identify the errors (if not, then it requires re-teaching). As Alex Quigley (2016) highlights:

> ...providing good examples may actually prove less useful than using contrasting examples that provide 'near misses' and 'not quite good enough'. By challenging students to identify the flaws in those 'near misses' we get them thinking hard about the exact qualities that define 'excellence'.

Comparative Modelling

If the purpose of modelling is to build more confidence and clarity in students before deliberate practice, then comparative modelling can be a very helpful means to ensure their understanding of what exactly a quality response will look like. The principle is, again, simple: provide a range of responses to a topic or question and ask students to rate them for their effectiveness and provide justification for their responses.

This also can be a useful way to illuminate different ways of approaching a task, addressing the notion that modelling may stifle our students' creativity. Andy Tharby and Shaun Allison (2015) suggest that it can open up a greater understanding about how to approach the task differently:

> Multiple modelling can also inspire creativity. In subjects such as Art and English, which often involve handing over the artistic licence to students, sharing more than one model allows us to demonstrate that successful outcomes might be very different.

Student Models

Completing exemplar responses all takes time; fortunately, the likelihood is that a strong model answer may well be hiding in the wings of your class. Even more importantly, it may well have the potential to inspire stronger responses than our own teacher-led modelling. Giving students the opportunity to reflect on what their peers are capable of can send out powerful psychological messages and raise aspiration levels.

Simply photocopying and distributing a strong student response to a task can often have more impact than repetitive marking comments. Again, we can seek to encourage young people to share their thoughts on what skills the example demonstrates. Even more interestingly, we can ask the individual themselves to talk to the class about the process of completing the work, refining exactly how they arrived at the successful end point. It all helps in assisting students' meta-cognitive capacity, more of which we will unpick in the next chapter.

Live and Collaborative Modelling

When John Tomsett, headteacher of Huntington school in York, realised his economics students lacked the ability to respond well in examination questions, he decided to model the whole process of 'what I think about when I am tackling an exam paper'. He completed the paper with added annotations of his thought process, then went through it with his students. As he outlines 'the ability of students to complete a different paper to a high standard was significant' (Tomsett, 2015).

This moves to an even more public level when we decide to actively complete a question in front of students. Again, the premise is extremely simple and requires little preparation: we take a question or essay that we want students to develop clarity over how to approach and we complete it 'live' in front of the students. This could be done on the whiteboard or using that most helpful of modelling tools: the visualiser. To avoid the possibility of a class being distracted while we undergo this, we question them at each stage: why have I done this? What is my next step? They can even complete the questions alongside us so that they have annotated notes for revision purposes.

Then, rather than being didactic, the modelling process becomes collaborative. Once we have talked through and discussed our rationale for approaching the task this way, students are then ready to attempt a similar task that requires the same skills.

There is an immense value in completing a task alongside students while they work. At times, our circulation of the room and discussions with students can only serve to distract them. To demonstrate the need for silent focus and concentration, sitting down and writing or completing tasks with students can visibly model focus and the shared process of learning. When students see you similarly immersed in focusing on a question, they are more likely to genuinely concentrate themselves. Any interruptions are quickly dealt with – 'quiet I am trying to concentrate!' The post-analysis can then involve sharing some students' work and sharing our own as well.

Modelling of Academic Discourse

In 2012, School 21 opened in East London and placed oracy at the core of its curriculum, with a mission statement that outlines how an oracy focus in the classroom can transform young people's lives. In our role as educators we also arguably have a moral imperative to equip young people with the strategies to ensure they leave school with the ability to communicate in a sophisticated and clear manner.

Talk in the classroom is like osmosis: if it is sloppy, vague, generic and careless then that diffuses into everything else. Classrooms are microcosms of the world, and in the world we are expected to communicate widely and appropriately with a diverse audience. If every school subject holds to four communication rules, with consistency throughout the school environment, then young people will develop as confident speakers. These are:

1. Answering all questions in full sentences.

2. Avoiding unnecessary fillers; for example, the ubiquitous 'like'.

3. Demonstrating knowledge of subject-appropriate and wider vocabulary at all times.

4. Speaking formally and appropriately at all times.

All of these require unpicking and further dialogue to rationalise their purpose with young people. The responsibility lies with teachers to model each of these four elements; they will not happen by magic. Slow and repetitive exposure to language will also improve students' ability to use the key words and subject-specific terminology that we want to see in their work. If we are curious about how we use language, if we seek to demonstrate the enormous potential and capacity of words – regardless of our subject area of speciality – students will join us in this mission towards eloquence.

The educational potential of modelling in improving understanding and outcomes is significant. To enable students to have a deeper conception of their own thinking and capacity to learn, however, requires us to unpick the intimidating mystery that is metacognition. In doing so, we can begin to examine what really motivates our students.

Slow Questions

1. Is your marking revealing significant misconceptions students have about how to structure and approach tasks?

2. Are you investing lesson time in sharing assessment criteria that is difficult for students to grasp?

3. What role does modelling play in your classroom now and could it be employed more?

4. Are you making your thinking explicit to students and deconstructing how to approach a task?

5. Could there be more scope for you to prepare a teacher model answer?

6. Are you confident about not marking work and instead providing students with a model to ensure clarity about how they should complete a task?

7. What opportunities are there to use student model answers in your lessons?

CHAPTER 11: DEVELOPING MOTIVATED AND REFLECTIVE LEARNERS

I doubt, therefore I think, I think therefore I am.
Rene Descartes

If we were given thirty minutes to construct our dream class, a class that would be our vision of perfection, what qualities would we want to dominate? In our frantic attempt to narrow this down, we might recall the students we have taught who have gone on to achieve wonderful things. Was their success necessarily a question of intellect? Or was it the down to the fact that they were driven, motivated and determined to achieve their very best?

We might then pause and reflect that to be driven is not quite enough; it is only one element that can assist in achievement. Drive needs to be combined with the ability to recognise the strengths and weaknesses of what we are doing; with the more unique qualities of reflection.

Utopian daydreaming, unfortunately, will not change the fact that these qualities only seem to magically manifest themselves in isolated pockets of our students. They are the students who we herald as 'gifted' and wax lyrically about their natural talents. There is, however, an alternative argument: as teachers, there is more we could do to cultivate both the capacity to reflect and the motivation of our students.

Invisible Thinking

One of the great mysteries of the classroom is the invisibility of student thinking. What is really going through their minds as they complete tasks? How are they monitoring their own knowledge and understanding? Despite our herculean efforts at the front of the room, why is it that some of the students we teach are woefully over-confident and so poor at judging what they know and don't know?

While we will never be able to peer into the murky world of their minds (nor would we particularly want to), there is much we can do in the classroom to influence our students' capacity to think about their learning. The issue is obvious: even if we desperately impart extensive facts and information into their minds, unless they have the capacity to think about how they can apply these effectively it is not going to assist them in learning. John Hattie (2012) argues that the 'teacher needs to know how each student thinks, and the thinking demands of each step in the lesson'. To achieve this, familiarising ourselves with different ways in which we can efficiently train students to think about their learning is a useful starting point.

Metacognition

Metacognition is one of those words that will often lurk intimidatingly in the background of debates about education. It is one which a great deal of us nod sagely at, while having no real understanding of what it is or why it might come in use (myself included!) Metacognition is not about making teachers dissolve and become irrelevant; rather, it is about providing tools to enable young people to learn in the future and assisting them in developing an awareness of the progress they are making.

By carefully and explicitly teaching metacognitive strategies, we assist in taking young people from their position of novices to experts; in effect, taking control of moving their learning forward. Doing this from a young age can facilitate their ability to develop lifelong learning habits, and become students who understand the connections between different tasks and then apply their thinking in different environments. To return to our utopian class ideal: it can help to develop what Dylan Wiliam (2016) defines as 'students as essential partners in the learning process'. Surely it is this that should be one of the residing qualities of any ideal class?

The Research

In a review of research, the Education Endowment Foundation (EEF), an independent charity set up in 2011 to improve educational attainment, stated (2017) that metacognition was the second highest impact strategy that teachers could use in the classroom. If we can develop students' ability to understand *why* they are doing things in particular ways, then we will help them to be able to apply these skills independently later on. Importantly, it will allow them to accurately self-assess their abilities, assisting with the process of effective revision that we will explore later.

Research has also shown that teaching 'critical thinking' subjects outside of the domain of our subjects does not have a lasting impact, often resulting in lost learning time. Instead, as Daniel Willingham (2007) notes, 'Critical thinking should be taught in the context of subject matter.'

Fast Thinking

In a society that provides thousands of opportunities to procrastinate, the ability to encourage reflection and avoid rushed thinking becomes challenging. In Daniel Kahneman's *Thinking, Fast and Slow* (2012), the author outlines that the human brain has two different modes of thinking when presented with information: System 1 and System 2. System 1 is our fast and automatic manner of thinking that requires little moderation or effort. System 2 is our attention and effortful mental activity, including agency, choice and concentration.

We all know students who seem to function only by using System 1 – they rush through work without any sense of care and attention. We frequently cajole them to take the time to proofread their work, to check over answers and not to finish unless they are sure that it represents their best work. Yet, often, these appeals seem to fall on deaf ears.

Metacognitive strategies can build young people's capacity to avoid rushed thinking and encourage them to slow down the thought processes. There is also the moral obligation: we want to set young people up with the capacity to think carefully as the strands of scaffolding are removed. Schools that lack this focus, and that teach only skills to secure examination results, are one of the reasons why so many students struggle as they move through university, with its increased demands on metacognitive awareness.

Cultivating Problem Solvers

Being equipped with the ability to solve a problem is essential in developing both reflective and motivated learners. Having a skill set to apply to problems means that young people are more likely to be optimistic about learning and to exert effort when grappling with challenging tasks.

Problem-solving skills, however, need to be actively taught throughout the curriculum. Solving a problem is a System 2, slow process of thinking ability: a skill that becomes like intuition for expert thinkers, but is very challenging for the novice thinker. There are three metacognitive steps we can take to build our students to be more confident problem solvers: planning, monitoring and evaluation.

1. Planning

When we face a problem, as intuitive and expert thinkers, we devise a step-by-step action plan for finding a resolution. This is often the process that young people and novice thinkers neglect in any subject; they want to dive straight into completing the final task, without any reflection. Alex Quigley (2016) suggests that 'We need to slow them down, breaking the task down, so they can reach a deeper level of understanding of what they need to do'.

To do this, students need an array of planning strategies at their disposal, and the ability to decide which planning method is most effective in supporting them to complete the task well. In order to understand the nuances of different methods, they need to be explicitly taught and given time to practise them. Daniel Willingham (2007) notes that 'You can teach students maxims about how they ought to think, but without background knowledge and practice, they probably will not be able to implement the advice they memorize'. Some planning strategies that we might seek to familiarise students with, so that they can automatically apply them in a future examination situation, are:

1. Mind maps

2. Venn Diagrams

3. Bullet points

4. Listing

5. Checklists

6. Concept maps.

Again, modelling is important here. At first, we can talk through the process and show students how we would plan for the task to help scaffold their own planning attempts. This can be used to create a series of learned questions that students can apply when faced with a similar task in the future. The more these questions are repeated with students, and the more they are tested on them, the more likely they are to be able to implement them independently. Examples include:

'What exactly is this task asking me to do?'

'What should I do first?'

'What prior knowledge do I need to complete the task effectively?'

'Which strategies will I use to help me to complete the task?'

'Are there any strategies that I have used before that might be useful?'

'Where might I go wrong with this task?'

'How much time will I need to complete the task effectively?

At this stage it would be useful to combine thinking in the class, to discuss different approaches and give students opportunities to rehearse how to complete the task effectively.

Using spot the difference strategies in the planning stage is also important. Unpicking questions with students and asking them to reflect on how they would plan for these varying styles of questioning will help them to understand exactly what the different expectations of them are. It will set them up with a clear understanding of the thinking they need to employ to answer different types of questions in more pressurised situations.

2. Monitoring

A plan will arm students with a strategy and an approach to the work they are completing. Yet, as with all aspects of demonstrating a skill, we need to be able to pause, reflect and question how effectively we are completing the task during the active practise phase.

When I failed my driving test for the first time at the tender age of thirty, it was primarily because of my inability to take a more objective approach to how I was driving. The plan was secure; my driving instructor had even given me a checklist to study the night before. Yet, when the day arrived, I wasn't confident enough, and anxiety meant that I blindly went through the test. As a novice I wasn't competent enough to monitor my driving independently (and I am still not, according to my wife). I still needed the scaffolds of my instructor to offer support and guidance.

Having a series of learned questions can encourage students to avoid the mindless completion of a task, and allow them to slow down their rate of activity. It will also help them to pause and consider how effectively they are making progress and allow them to make changes to their work, helping them to become more objective about the work they are completing. Some examples of these learned questions are:

Am I on the right track?

What am I doing well?

What do I need to do more of?

Do I need to do something differently?

Am I following my plan?

Do I need to speed up or slow down to complete the task in time?

These questions will need to be repeated and tested over time to ensure retention. Often, this can be as simple as a 'check-in' during the deliberate practice phase. As an English teacher, I try to get each class to complete a piece of extended writing every week. Every fifteen minutes or so during these tasks, I will build in a 'check-in' point that ensures that students reflect back on their plan and consider how effectively they are completing the task.

Having a timer on the whiteboard is another simple way to help students regulate their own progress and develop the ability to reflect on where they should be after a certain amount of time has gone by. Peps Mccrea (2017) notes that 'check-ins' can provide a helpful way to 'build attentional awareness'. Initially this requires a trigger, such as 'set an alarm to go off at 15 minutes or so intervals during your lesson'. At this point students 'check in': they make a quick note of what they have been thinking about, and then get straight back to what they were doing'. This teaches students to be concerned with accuracy and refining their work as they complete it, traits that are important in any subject in the curriculum.

3. Evaluation

As we shall see, there is a worrying and blind reliance on feedback from young people. They quickly pass on the ownership of a piece of work to a teacher as soon as it is complete. This means that we often battle against poorly constructed and rushed work when we mark; mindlessly completed work that demonstrates little or no reflection. Even more frustratingly, when the work is returned the student then glances for a grade and quickly moves on, unless the feedback is engineered to secure an active response from the student in question. By making it easy for them to find out externally how they have done with a task, we lose the opportunity to hone reflective abilities for their future learning. In effect, we drive young people not towards independent thinking, but towards compliance and laziness.

Instead, if we can train them to evaluate their work carefully before they pass it to us, then the benefits are immense: less time marking and better ownership of work from students. By being relentless with this, we are empowering young people for their future independence in the workplace, where if their work is not considered good enough they will achieve little.

There should always be an evaluation step in place before we accept work from students. Again, the frequent repetition of key questions for students to apply can assist in ensuring that this becomes a process they are used to undertaking after they complete a task. At times, asking students to write their responses to these answers can also help us to inform our future planning, as we can clearly see where they have struggled with the task:

What have I learned from completing this task?

What are my strengths – what did I do well?

Did I use my plan effectively?

What are my weaknesses – what do I need to prioritise doing next?

When could I use this kind of thinking again?

Does this represent my very best work? If not, what do I need to change?

The Resilient and Motivated Learner

Building motivation and engagement with learning is more than platitudes and posters; it is about filtering effort and resilience through all aspects of school life. This is driven, in part, by the ethos of a leadership team: are they modelling high expectations and a ubiquitous drive for achievement? It is also about taking frequent opportunities to discuss the challenges of learning and the benefits of perseverance with young people.

In our individual classrooms, it is about coaching scholarly behaviours from students: modelling how to overcome moments in learning where we encounter difficulties. Case studies are useful to deconstruct: Thomas Edison's maxim 'I haven't failed, I've just found 10,000 ways that won't work' is a reassuring focus for those who can't grasp that troublesome maths question! Using peer modelling to encourage young people to talk through their mechanisms for overcoming difficulty will nourish this, as will our own learning behaviours in the classroom. The more we vocalise our own thinking, our own struggles with learning and our own passion for our subjects, the more chance there is that young people will join us on that journey.

The Big Picture

When we have a conception of what we are working towards and why, it becomes easier to persevere with tasks. If students cannot see the value in what they are working on, it is common sense to argue that they will invest less energy in accomplishing the task and be less motivated. As teachers, our daily battles with a troublesome Year 11 group are easy to keep in perspective when we recognise that we are playing a role of real importance in securing their futures.

While we can inspire our students through the force of our enthusiasm, personality and the relationships we form with them, clearly outlining the benefit of doing the task in relation to the bigger picture will (hopefully) result in them investing more effort. This will also allow students to perceive the gaps in their learning, and see what it is they are working towards. Then they can begin to internalise a plan of action to help them arrive at this point, with clear and practical goals put in place.

These may be short-term goals, such as to grasping to do long division effectively, or long-term goals, such as to preparing them to write a detailed analytical essay. Removing the examination and level obsession is also enabling for young people; showing them how a particular skill will help them outside of school can rationalise battling through a topic that is not ostensibly engaging. We may well encourage students to set smaller, more attainable goals themselves so that they can start to take ownership of their progress.

No matter how sophisticated students become in their employment of metacognitive strategies, and no matter how motivated and driven they are to do well, they remain in the position of the novice learner in the classroom. Any novice requires suitable feedback; feedback that they can couple with their own understanding in order to recognise how to improve. The next chapter will tackle that most time-devouring of teacher tasks: providing feedback.

Slow Questions

1. Are you reflecting on ways to improve your students' ability to consider their own thinking?

2. Are there more opportunities in lessons to model your thinking about how to approach tasks with students?

3. Is time designated in lessons to give students opportunities to plan out how they will approach a task? Are they aware of the strategies they can use to do this?

4. What steps are you taking to ensure that students are pausing and considering how well they are completing a task?

5. Is there time at the end of each task for students to evaluate how well it has been completed and make changes?

6. Are you exploring both resilience and motivation with your students, and making it a real focus in your interactions with them?

CHAPTER 12: DEBUNKING MANIC MARKING

Insanity: doing the same thing over and over again and expecting different results.
Albert Einstein

Our bleary, bloodshot eyes glance at the clock: 10pm. Stiff hands place down the highlighter and different coloured pens and reach desperately for another strong cup of coffee. The intimidating collection of books beside us laughs cruelly; with a taunting sneer, they appear to adopt the voice of our performance manager: 'Senior management are out on the prowl tomorrow. Remember the two-week marking cycle we agreed on. Remember the different coloured pens we mark in. Deep mark. Deep mark.'

Mindless Marking

Is there a more thoughtless aspect of teaching than marking? Is there anything that de-intellectualises the profession and reduces us to mindless cog in the machine than the slavish and repetitive process of providing endless comments on work? Given the external accountability and demands on our time, is there anything we do with more speed and less reflection than mark a set of workbooks?

Fear not, this will not be yet another pointless and enraged diatribe against feedback. Feedback and marking are both essential in ensuring that we are teaching our students effectively. Proactive solutions to the issue of their impact is what we need to focus on, alongside deepening our understanding of when and how feedback is effective and efficient. Marking is one vastly overrated branch of the feedback family tree; one that seeks to steal the limelight and dominate the headlines. And, dominate the headlines it does, for all the wrong reasons.

Marking and Workload

In a recent survey of thousands of teachers by *The Guardian* (2016), 82% of respondents suggested that their workload was unmanageable. Even more alarmingly, the same survey highlighted that almost half of the teachers surveyed intended to leave the profession after five years. While clearly there are numerous factors that will contribute to this, marking and workload issues appear to be intrinsically united. In the Department of Education's 2014 Workload challenge, which used over 44,000 responses from teachers, marking was highlighted as the single biggest contributor to unsustainable workload. Marking, it would appear, is repelling teachers from the profession.

For the busy teacher on a full timetable, this comes as no surprise. When we combine our classes, there are industrial levels of books to plough through and constantly shifting school policies to be rigidly adhered to. This is coupled with what has become the ubiquitous threat of 'workbook reviews'.

Workbook reviews are often poorly executed; ironically, due to time pressures on management, they are cursively glanced at when they are 'reviewed'. The result is that these reviews look only at the scope and amount of teacher feedback given, without any conversation about whether or not a student is improving in the key skills required for the subject. Instead of a focus on learning, they feed the irrational 'marking warrior' spirit of those who loudly declaim that they have been up until all hours marking, and whose books appear to be resplendent in multi-coloured marking. They perpetrate the glorification of busy marking – the automatic assumption that if we are marking a significant amount we are, by default, moving forward the learning of our students.

The Research

This marking mania becomes more ludicrous when we see that there is little robust and meaningful research available on the impact of written marking on student progress. Indeed, research has hinted that the disproportionate amount of time teachers spend marking work does not result in equal learning gains.

The Independent Teacher Workload Review Group (2016) noted that quantity is being blurred with quality, and highlighted that professional judgement is integral in achieving effective marking that is 'meaningful, manageable and motivating'. Professional judgement, however, is not at the heart of most schools' marking policies. In fact, it is undermined, and in the worst cases, implicitly removed by the prescriptive nature of marking cycles.

This is not an argument for the removal of all marking, or to ignore the importance of students receiving written feedback. A slower, less-is-more solution can assist us in making marking more efficient and impactful. By taking this approach, we will also move away from the erroneous identification of marking as the main form of feedback. This is feedback philosophy at

Michaela School in central London. Here they have, for the most part, done away with written feedback. Instead, as highlighted in *Battle Hymn of the Tiger Teachers*, 'When Michaela pupils write, they receive feedback the next day. We can give such swift feedback because we don't mark' (Birbalsingh, 2016). The school gives scope and time to exploring the range of other mechanisms that provide useful feedback: self-assessment, peer assessment and verbal feedback.

The Purpose

For feedback to be meaningful, we need to be clear on our rationale for investing time in it. The same is true in our discussions with students; they need to be clear why we are investing so much of our time in providing them with guidance. Feedback is important in any learning cycle, as it closes the gaps between current and desired performance. No matter how reflective an individual is, it is difficult for them to make improvements without the clarity of feedback from someone more experienced.

When done well, feedback should continue to drive students towards self-regulation and ownership of their learning. There is also the human factor; it is clear that feedback assists in building relationships with students. When we make clear our investment in their work, it demonstrates how important it is to us that they do well. It motivates them to continue to persevere, particularly when we can build a productive feedback dialogue with them.

Pre-marking Self-assessment

Demonstrating high expectations through marking happens long before we receive a piece of student work. We have already noted the frustration we feel when we know we are marking substandard work, ploughing through what is clearly not our students' best efforts. Effective teaching steps that we have explored earlier can be employed to ensure the quality of what ends up on our marking pile: efficient instruction, questioning to ensure understanding and modelling what excellent performance looks like. All this will help to ensure that students know exactly where they are going with the task, meaning that they will be able to engage more with the feedback that is provided.

The thorough self-assessment is the final part of this process. It is vital that young people take ownership of their piece of work, that they go through the process of checking it carefully and that they are proud to submit it for our scrutiny. This self-assessment can be aided using a simple 'Checklist of Excellence' approach, shared with students after they have completed the task:

1. Does this work represent the very best of your ability?

2. Have you read over and checked your work?

3. Does your work showcase good presentation?

4. Have you reflected on what steps you have taken with the work?

5. What do you think are your strengths and weaknesses?

While useful as a framework, these are merely words – for them to have impact, they need to be rigorously applied. Young people need to appreciate that time invested in marking is sacred; if they hand in work that does not reach the best they are capable of, they should be asked to repeat it. The moment we accept rushed work, we deliver a message about our own expectations and standards. We are also signing away long evenings to mindless marking of mediocre work.

Before Marking

Our first speed-induced error with marking is we don't apply strategic thinking to the process. We might have a marking schedule that tells us when we have allocated time to marking our classes' books, but this is merely perpetuating the hamster wheel approach to marking. It is simply impossible, regardless of what subject we teach, to provide young people with useful feedback for everything they do in the classroom. Attempting to do so will, at best, result in extensive superficial marking or, at worst, consign ourselves to an early marking grade.

What we need to do is be selective; to map out what work will receive feedback from us, and why. This requires consideration to make sure that we are not overwhelmed with work to mark, which is why we need to plan out our time, be judicious and reflective. All classroom teachers are all to guiltily aware that the quicker students receive feedback on a task, the more effective it is. It seems rather obvious: if we hand in our work, then wait weeks to get it back we lose the investment in the task. Some questions to consider when deciding what to mark:

1. What are the skills that I want young people to have secured?

2. What will I not be commenting on in this marking?

3. What will they do as a result of me marking this work?

4. Do my students know what excellence looks like in this task?

5. Do I know exactly what a strong response is?

We need to be secure about exactly what the rationale for marking is, as we don't want to overwhelm students by commenting on every aspect of their work. All this will do is lead to 'red pen fear' and demotivate them in their desire to improve. We want to filter, simplify and focus on the skills that need to be developed. The fifth question above, regarding our own knowledge of what a strong response looks like, might seem condescending. However, we cannot mark our students' work effectively unless we, as the expert, have complete ownership of what we are looking for.

In my first year of teaching A-level English Literature, I slogged over endless essays without seeing any visible improvement. The issue was that, as a novice approaching the exam specification, I didn't know exactly what I was marking for. I was as perplexed as the students by the baffling assessment requirements. This is why teaching new specifications is so stressful – our benchmark for excellence is hazy. The more dialogue we can have with colleagues, and the more useful collaboration and sharing we can do to inform our understanding, the more chance our feedback will be productive for students.

During Marking

So, we have a piece that reflects our students' best efforts that they have carefully worked towards. If our plan is to mark their work and get it back to them by the next lesson, we have asked them to hand in their books on the beginning page that will be marked from (a nifty, time-saving device). In the spirit of clarity and rationalising our feedback with students, we have explained to them that we will not be reading the work that has built up to whatever we will be marking in more depth. In reality there is no impact at all in cursive ticking or writing 'good' on a piece of work; it is time that is utterly wasted. We need our students to be clear that this work still matters, but that it is part of a process that results in specific feedback on one identified piece of work.

Rather than delving straight in with the red wand at this stage, it is helpful to read over a few examples from the class first. Reading a sample will illustrate what some of the misconceptions the whole class may have that might be that will need addressed. It is here where we can construct the beginnings of our target list: a set of numbered codes related to targets that we will share with students when the work is returned to them. This can be applied in any subject for any skill.

Instead of repetitively writing the same comment in ten out of thirty workbooks, we assign a number to that comment. If, for example, I am marking an essay where I might have to repeatedly draw a student's attention to using more textual evidence, I would assign this a number (such as, '1'), then write down a '1' at the end of their work. By writing out this target themselves, the student is forced to engage more with the feedback than they would with a cursory glance at the end of the page.

Next, we make use of codes to define areas of need in the body of the piece of marked work. As the EEF report (2017) identifies, there is 'no difference between the effectiveness of coded or un-coded feedback'. Usually, a school's marking policy will include codes to use for effectiveness. If not, create and share these with students for clarity.

Time invested in marking needs to lead to dialogue with students; it has to be seen as part of a wider process. The easiest way to remind ourselves of the conversations we will need to have is to write notes on a separate sheet as we mark. This can range from praise to specific areas of need that will not be addressed by writing a comment. This then becomes our guide for conversations we will have with individual students and the whole class in the next lesson. Again, slowing down our process will have time saving implications; we can be more thoughtful about what we will write down and what will be given as verbal feedback to students.

Again, it is important to reflect on how a comment we are writing will be interpreted or received by a young person. The reality is that much of what we write while marking will not help move learning forward or be motivational. Vague and generic praise, such as the use of 'good', does not make it clearer why something is effective. Telling a student they need to include a 'wider range of vocabulary' will not help them. Common sense suggests if they knew how to do this, they would have included it in their first attempt at the work.

Instead, framing the feedback as instructional, while keeping it as sparse and specific as possible, will provide them with clear and definitive ways of moving their work forward. The above request for more vocabulary then becomes 'What three words could you add here?' This means the student has to think, reflect, then add in changes to their work.

Grading Conundrums

Offering a mark and a grade on students' work is another area in which care is required. If we provide a grade, the danger is that our students will quickly look at it, and then will not invest time in improving it. Grades have an indication of finality: representing closure and the neat ending of a unit. When it comes to end of unit assessments or mock examinations then it makes sense; if not, it is useful to award marks and grades more sparingly.

Post-Marking

There is a maxim that should always be applied to written feedback: students need to spend significantly more time acting on the feedback than we do giving it. That is why it is vital that we coach young people to receive feedback appropriately. By making our feedback lean, instructional and clear we can make this difficult process more manageable for young people.

Too often 'response to marking' lessons are lacking in clear management and direction. To be a valuable use of lesson time, students need absolute clarity about what they need to do and how it will benefit their learning. To ensure the feedback loop is complete, young people need to be shown how to respond to marking effectively. In the initial stages with a class, this will need to be slow and painstaking; again, modelling how we expect them to use the feedback.

For our feedback to have impact, we need to work hard to create a culture in which there is openness to trial and error and continuous improvement. Less confident students can begin to instantly shut down when they are on the receiving end of what they construe to be negative feedback. We need to encourage students to see errors as things that are exciting, things that can move them forward into a deeper understanding and mastery of the content.

Whole-class Feedback

Whole-class feedback is a vital part of this feedback loop. Here we can take time to unpick the targets we have constructed, asking students to justify why we have come up with them. There may be elements of the work here in which we deliberately slow the pace and re-teach a skill that students have clearly not mastered. There is no point in them starting to instantly respond to comments if it is just going to lead to reiterating misconceptions.

To avoid this, we can also showcase excellent examples from students themselves, taking time to unpick them and assist those students who haven't been as successful in their understanding of how their work can improve. A visualiser can be extremely useful here, avoiding the need to invest time in photocopying lots of student work.

Student Response

Once we have gone over whole-class targets, we need to give ample time for students to act on the feedback. Again, it is important to rationalise this approach with young people and to explain that we get better at something by trial and error. My favourite examples, from an English teacher's perspective, are using models of George Orwell redrafting his writing, or showing extracts of how J.K. Rowling changed earlier drafts of her *Harry Potter* books. No doubt each school subject has their own version of J.K. Rowling: an example that can be used to highlight the craft of meticulous attention to detail that ensures improvement. Then, it is important that students have the time to reflect and improve their work based on our feedback. It is now that we can circulate the room and have as many conversations with students as possible about their work.

Redrafting or 'upgrading' the marked work is one way to approach this, visibly allowing students to demonstrate how they have moved forward in their thinking. This involves taking a section or the whole piece of work and repeating it, building in comments and targets. It is important to monitor this process to ensure that the improved response moves from beyond shallow and superficial layers of development; otherwise, the response becomes merely about performance. Regardless, asking the student to articulate what steps they have made to improve their work will help to ensure this knowledge is secure and can be applied at a later date.

The real skill is the notion of continuous development. Can students then apply the feedback in a similar task? This will help in ensuring that learning has 'stuck' as a result of feedback.

Peer Assessment

In Graham Nuthall's *The Hidden Lives of Learners* (2007), the author revealed that in his observations, 80% of verbal feedback came from peers and that a significant amount of it is wrong. Since then peer assessment has received much criticism as a way of using feedback. Indeed, there are questionable practices. Asking students to 'mark' each other's work, without any scaffolding, modelling or support, will only lead to the inevitable praise or vague comments that they bestow upon each other: 'your work is fantastic' or 'your presentation is lovely!'

Like everything in the classroom, for peer assessment to be an efficient use of lesson time it needs training, clarity and guidance. The peer assessment I have found most useful is employing techniques from 'Gallery Critique' from Ron Berger's *An Ethic of Excellence* (2003). This enables young people to see what they are capable of doing throughout the class and makes them more likely to grasp the different ways a task can be approached. To do this efficiently involves encouraging young people to provide clear feedback using the following steps that Shaun Allison and Andy Tharby make use of in *Making Every Lesson Count* (2015):

1. Something kind: I really like the way you.../Excellent use of.../The most successful thing about this was..

2. Something specific: In the first/second/third paragraph you.../Your point here was difficult to understand because.../Your sentence, paragraph, point here is...

3. Something helpful: Think about adding.../Think about taking away.../Have you thought about.../You could improve this by...

The more that students are trained in completing tasks like this, the less chance there is of peer assessment being wasted lesson time. Instead, it becomes a powerful way to encourage students to recognise the qualities of good work and how to reach those standards.

Feedback deserves a similar microscopic level of detailed reflection and experimentation as with all aspects of teaching. We have to discover what works in moving our students forward. Inevitably, we must work within the constraints of a school policy; this being said, if we can visibly demonstrate how the learning is improving students' work, then we are doing our work efficiently.

By being strategic about what we mark, clear and concise with comments we provide and training students to respond effectively, we begin to impact more on students' progress than our own exhaustion levels. Endlessly repeating the same tired marking methods will only further isolate those who are struggling and demotivated in our profession. Ofsted, after all, in their 2015 report 'Myths' highlighted that 'it did not expect to see any specific frequency, type or volume of marking and feedback'. That statement appears to me to be a beckoning call to wrestle back control and begin to use our professional judgement when it comes to how, and when, we mark.

Slow Questions

1. Are you becoming another victim of mindless marking fervour?

2. Is there a more strategic approach you could take in deciding what to mark and when?

3. Are you emphasising the sacred nature of marking and giving students time to construct a detailed self-assessment?

4. Is your written feedback to students sparse and instructional?

5. How much effort is going into training your students on how to respond to feedback?

6. Could you look at building in more structured examples of peer assessment?

CHAPTER 13: MEMORY MYSTERIES

The sweet sweet memories you give- a me
You can't beat the memories you give-a me.
'Memories are Made of This'
Dean Martin

Is there ever a time where the amount of information and the diversity of knowledge we need to remember is as overwhelming as during our secondary education? It is the first real cognitively demanding period of your life: with a huge cast of teachers urging you to remember the vital elements of their subjects.

While we do all we can to try to drill our learning tourists into retaining the knowledge they need, as a profession we invest little time reflecting on the mystery of memory. A strategic, whole school approach to support effective teaching for memory is certainly not gracing the classrooms of many schools; we are far too busy with more immediately pressing concerns to consider it. To neglect it, however, is to leave us without a fundamental grasp of how learning takes place. As Peps Mccrea (2017) argues in his opening to *Memorable Teaching*, 'memory underpins learning'.

Learning vs Performance
The best place to start this investigation into memory is to question how we know if a student has really learned anything in our class. Nicholas C. Soderstrom and Robert A. Bjork (2015) call this the 'distinction between learning and performance'. This observation indicates that it is challenging to find clarity about how effectively information is stored in our students' memory. Are we confident that we know when our students have really grasped something, or are they simply replicating for us exactly what they think we want to hear? Furthermore, as Soderstrom and Bjork (2015) suggest:

> Performance is often fleeting and, consequently, a highly imperfect index of learning does not appear to be appreciated by learners or

instructors who frequently misinterpret short-term performance as a guide to long-term learning.

Learning is not what students can do at a particular moment in time; instead, it is what they can replicate the next week, the next term and six months down the line. Paul Kirschner *et al* (2006) have argued this forcefully stating that, 'If nothing has changed in long-term memory, nothing has been learned'. The reality is that grasping the complexity of how to secure information in our students' memory will transform our lessons from superficial and surface level learning, to teachers who can embed knowledge skilfully.

The mind is a mysterious engine, and for our purposes as educators we don't often delve into its inner workings. Both the long- and short-term memory are what we need to be most thoughtful about in our teaching.

Long-Term Memory

This is the gold mine of memory that we want to secure for our students. Our long-term memory retains information and skills that we can access to make sense of the world around us. There are three distinct types: procedural memory (knowledge of how to do things, such as ride a bicycle); semantic memory (storing factual information); and episodic memory (episodes that we have experienced in our lives). In the classroom it is predominantly the semantic memory that we are looking to develop with our students.

Working Memory

This is our short-term memory; it is our capacity to hold information in our minds over short periods of time. When we meet someone for the first time our working memory kicks in so that we can remember their name and avoid any embarrassment. When we give instructions to students, it is their working memory that we are relying on to ensure they complete the instructions.

Forgetting

The added difficulty of supporting our students' ability to retain information is just how quickly young people forget things. We all experience the daily struggles of this in our classroom, such as occasions when things we felt were completely secure in our students' minds appear to have completely vanished the following day. The ominous forgetting curve, which has appeared in various manifestations since it was initially introduced by Hermann Ebbinghaus' experiments in 1885, illustrates this point. The forgetting curve identifies that learning reduces at a diminishing rate over time unless it is consciously reviewed. Also, as Graham Nutthall (2007) notes, 'as learning occurs so does forgetting'. Our students may look like they have grasped the concepts we have explored with them in the immediate present, but the likelihood is that they will forget it quickly.

Without revisiting learned information periodically, our hours of heroic endeavours to secure knowledge will have been in vain. Ideally, we should have an array of strategies in our (long-term!) memories that we can employ to conquer the forgetting curve's ominous curse.

Desirable Difficulties

Robert Bjork coined the phrase 'Desirable Difficulties' arguing that learning is required to be harder initially to make it easier to recall at a later time. (Bjork: 1994) While this has the impact of slowing down learning for students and increasing the level of challenge, it means that it is more likely to be retained at a later point. The following strategies have this philosophy at their core: challenging but effective for retention.

Connect with Prior Knowledge

The first method of inspiring more memory retention is by connecting new learning to what students already know – what E.D Hirsch (1996) described as 'the mental scaffolding and velcro to catch hold of what is going on'. This is the deep prior knowledge that is already embedded in young people's minds and can help them to access new material. Peps Mccrea (2017) calls this 'Priming': completing a pre-review to identify what they already know about a topic. As he writes 'Priming for learning is a bit like priming for painting. We prepare the surface to help our material stick better'.

Remembering something is challenging if it is lacking in a meaning that we can grasp, or if it is not linked to other aspects of a topic that we have some conception of. Giving students the opportunity to connect to prior knowledge will help to make their learning memorable. Elizabeth and Robert Bjork (2011) have summarised this as follows – 'We encode and store new information by relating it to what we already know – that is, by mapping it on to, and linking it up with, information that already exists in our memories'.

Some ways to use this in lessons:

1. Empty vessels: Give students a blank sheet of paper and ask them to write everything they can about a topic.

2. This reminds me of...: Introduce a new topic and ask students to consider what connections they could make to previous topics.

3. Connection map: Create a mind map for students to link the different topics and ideas explored.

4. Image-led discussion: Use images to lead into a discussion on the topic and link this back to prior understanding.

5. Use the cognitive impact of the simple question: Why? Asking students to reflect on why something is true will help them to draw out connections.

6. Start with: what do you remember about? This might take the form of a short test style unit that begins to make connections to previous learning.

Embrace Testing

Utter the dreaded word 'test' to most young people and there will be groans and howls of derision. Testing is synonymous with stress, pressure and high stakes. Even for us, as teachers, it often appears to serve only the simple purpose of grading and assessing students. Yet, testing could have transformable results in our quest to ensure our students can retain the information we want them to.

We have already seen that racing blindly through content, without returning to it periodically, will result in students forgetting important information. The benefits of testing can be numerous; as Henry L. Roediger *et al* (2011) have highlighted 'Tests can serve other purposes in educational settings that greatly improve performance'. When we move away from a 'test' that concludes a unit of work, we can instead introduce a repetitive, carefully planned structure of testing that removes the fear and stress factor.

Regular low-stakes quizzes (which are low in stress levels and don't impact on final grades) can be an excellent means of questioning students on their knowledge of a topic. What this requires them to do is actively search their memories to retrieve information in order to answer the questions. To be most effective, quizzes need to involve reflection and deeper thought, moving beyond the superficial retrieval of information. This avoids the speedy planning trap of 'practice, practice, practice', followed by an obligatory assessment bolted on at the end of a unit, and the subsequent race through the curriculum. It is also simple to prepare these and once we have a series of tests for a unit, we can use them again when we return to it in future years.

The other benefit of regular testing is that it identifies gaps in knowledge that can then be actively addressed, highlighting the areas that students need to invest more time in. This avoids the shock that mock examinations or assessments reveal at the end of the unit, when we gain an insight into the misconceptions that are dominating students' work. It gives us more ownership and more control over the direction of our teaching.

When testing because a normalised routine in lessons, the impact is also positive for students. By regularly getting the opportunity to see how well they are progressing through a unit, they can inform their own work outside of lessons, improving their ability to take ownership and monitor their own learning. The key, however, is to make sure that they are anxiety-free, keeping them light-hearted and embedding them in classroom routines. Some ways to employ testing and active retrieval in the classroom can include:

1. Regular recaps: These may take the form of a weekly or fortnightly quiz regarding important content that students need to know.

2. Starter testing: Students enter the classroom to a selection of questions on a PowerPoint that recap on previous content. Once this becomes routine students become much more focussed on trying to hold on knowledge from the previous lesson – their intellectual credence depends on it!

3. Plenary passes: Same as above, students need to answer questions correctly to exit the lesson.

4. Quizzes during lessons: One way to ensure students focus and listen during lessons is to tell them that at any point in the lesson they will be quizzed on what has just happened, without any notes. This can be as simple as giving students mini whiteboards to use to hold up what they believe is the right answer.

5. Quiz cards: Interactive way for students to test each other on a topic. They could be made by students and then employed in pairs.

Interleave

Why would we confuse students by switching between different topics and units? We could risk both demotivating and disengaging them as they struggle to switch their conceptual thinking between differing ideas. Yet interleaving, the challenging process of practising two or more subjects or skills, can have a powerful impact on learning. As Peter C Brown *et al* (2014) have noted:

The learning from interleaved practice feels slower than learning from massed practice... As a result, interleaving is unpopular and seldom used. Teachers dislike it because it feels sluggish... But the research shows unequivocally that mastery and long-term retention are much better if you interleave practice than if you mass it.

Again, it is common sense. If we teach a topic for weeks then don't return to it for six months, the chances of students recalling it in any real detail are slim. Instead, our strategic planning should be building in opportunities to mix up the content of the curriculum over a space of weeks and interleave different areas of study. This periodic returning to information means the memory is strengthened and it is less likely to result in students forgetting. Building routine and ensuring there is a quick method to check students' responses will also help to make this useful for them. Some strategies:

1. Rather than focusing entirely on a topic-by-topic approach, build in links back to previous learning.

2. Use quizzes to link back to previous points and information explored.

3. Interleave 'check in' moments, in which you flash up questions about a previous topic.

4. Have fortnightly/monthly interleave quizzes.

5. Topic tangent: introduce moments in lessons in which students switch quickly to a different topic and complete questions on it.

Streamline Learning

John Sweller's (1988) 'cognitive load theory' is an evaluation of how we should plan lessons and avoid overloading students. One of the important aims in developing the strength of the memory of our students is to avoid excessive cognitive burden. If we do overload their thinking in lessons, they become frustrated and lose the ability to hold on to the essential information they need to remember.

If we don't achieve this delicate balance – the optimum cognitive state – then we overpower our students' working memories, and by doing this we can negatively impact both their understanding and motivation. Instead, as Paul Kirschner suggests:

The simplest answer is to create learning tasks that are of the proper level of complexity depending on the student's prior knowledge and skills and then make use of techniques that require as little extraneous mental effort as you possible can (Hendrick and Macpherson, 2017).

We have already explored how quickly young people can be distracted from the fundamental purpose of learning, and how their vulnerable attention spans can be split in numerous different ways. We have also seen that, at times, our expert bias can make it difficult for us to fully appreciate the challenges that students may face with learning. Streamlining our teaching, cutting out anything superfluous that detracts from the learning we are seeking to encourage, will go a long way in curbing unproductive distractions. Here are some practical tips for the classroom:

1. Teach in small chunks, as this allows students to grasp how to complete a specific aspect of the learning, building motivation before moving on to the next task. These can increase in complexity and challenge as you move through lessons.

2. Give students time to both process information and ask questions to clarify their understanding; points about 'wait time' (see Chapter 6) come to the fore here.

3. Avoid unnecessary images and unrelated information if using PowerPoint slides. Instead, make sure everything is relevant to the learning outcomes of the lesson. As Graham Nuthall (2007) points out 'activities need careful designing so that students cannot avoid interacting with relevant information'.

4. Break down instructions into chunks, checking in with students during the instructions to ensure they are following exactly what we need them to do.

5. Give models so that it is clear what you want students to do and the skills you want them to replicate.

Repetition

Young people need multiple exposures to information in order to retain it; often, many more exposures than we might consider initially in our lesson planning. There is, of course, an element of repeated drill in the classroom. We constantly have to come back to key ideas and concepts to make sure that students are absolutely clear on how to approach tasks; however, this has the added bonus of strengthening their memories in the process. As we have already seen, we need to be secure on the key concepts and ideas that we will need to repeat with students in order to secure their understanding. Some strategies to employ:

1. Use plenaries at the end of the lesson to repeat the key learning that you want students to leave with.

2. Use testing to repeat key concepts that you want students to be clear on.

3. Give students opportunities for repeated practice of skills.

4. Use the probing questions strategies to make sure that students have complete clarity of the knowledge we are looking to secure.

5. Use whole-class repetition strategies. Students can vocally repeat definitions to help secure them in their memories. Tom Sherrington (2017) calls this 'choral chanting' and suggests that 'you guide students as they practise saying things out loud'. This can also be lots of fun for students; younger classes are particularly prone to getting rather involved!

Deliberate Practice

In order for students to understand exactly how to implement their learning, they need opportunities to practise the skills. Mastering a skill, as Barak Rosenshine (2012) highlights, requires extensive practice: 'Students need additional time to rephrase, elaborate and summarise new material in order to store it in their long-term memory. More successful teachers build in time for this'. Our lessons should always encompass time for individual practice, ideally in silent conditions, to ensure that our students are completely clear on exactly how to implement what they have been taught throughout the lesson.

Mnemonics

It is particularly challenging to remember something that is less tangible and obvious. Mnemonics can be an excellent technique to trigger memory cues for young people. Daniel Willingham (2009) notes that 'Mnemonics make meaningless material more meaningful, giving you something to think about and a good cue'.

Mnemonics can be applied across all subjects and for different purposes, but are particularly effective to help students to remember sequential information. I try to simplify the complexity of writing well about Shakespeare with the acrostic mnemonic 'SEAL' (Shakespeare, evidence, audience, language). If students achieve all of the elements in their analytical writing, they get the 'SEAL' of approval. Mathematics teachers often tackle complex sums with 'BODMAS' (bracket, over, division, multiplication, addition, subtraction). The impact of both is to streamline and focus students' thinking, when they are being asked to do something complex and potentially overwhelming.

I can still remember the way my geography teacher employed 'NESW' to help us remember the sequential nature of a compass (Never eat Shredded Wheat). All have at their heart a memorable phrase that breaks the content down, assisting students in the process of recalling information and making it memorable.

Clearly, all of the strategies in this chapter require us to make memory a real focus in our planning and in our everyday dialogue with students. Doing so will provide our students with the tools to do achieve well in their immediate exam-based future, but also enabling them to thrive as a learner throughout their lives. As we have seen, learning and memory are intrinsically bound up, and one cannot occur without the other.

While teaching for memory may well be one of the most complex explorations in this book, it is one that is superfluous unless young people have the capacity to translate their knowledge into a response and outcomes. To do this, regardless of the subject, literacy skills are utterly vital.

Slow Questions

1. Are you considering memory in your planning and teaching on a daily basis?

2. Are there more opportunities to employ the power of testing in your lessons?

3. Are you falling into the 'speedy content' trap, racing through without returning to check understanding and interleave content?

4. Are you allowing time for deliberate repetition of skills, and giving students plenty of opportunity to practice?

5. What potential is there for streamlining your lessons to provide complete clarity for your students?

6. Are you being reflective about cognitive overload in your lessons?

7. What potential could mnemonics have to aid students' memories in your subjects?

CHAPTER 14: LITERACY: BEYOND THE QUICK FIX SOLUTIONS

The secret to literacy is making the implicit explicit.
Geoff Barton

The word 'literacy' doesn't often inspire the most effusive reaction from teachers. In reality, a mere mention of the phrase often leads to an exaggerated yawn, undisguised indifference, and shouts of 'another literacy training session!' from colleagues. The ambivalence that, as Geoff Barton (2011) suggests, certainly doesn't evoke 'a spontaneous round of applause'. Another common response is the inevitable mocking of the failure of English teachers (or, even more extreme, the individual literacy coordinator) to do enough to secure literacy skills across the school.

The Collective Literacy Mission

As we shall see, such hastily formed judgements are misplaced. Literacy is absolutely imperative to the understanding and success of students in any subject. Not giving it the collective focus and drive that it needs is, arguably, to widen entrenched societal inequalities. This chapter will embrace the wisdom of George Sampson (1922), one of the first school inspectors, who passionately declared that 'Every teacher in English is a teacher of English'. We all have an important and collective part to play in the literacy mission.

The converse of this unified approach – leaving the ownership of all things literacy-related in the hands of a literacy coordinator – means fighting a noble, if exhausting and isolating, battle. The scope of what is deemed to be literacy is huge: reading, writing, spelling and speaking and listening are all commonly referred to as 'literacy skills'. Common sense dictates that just about all of these skills are integral in most lessons on a school curriculum. While having an individual who has a wealth of knowledge, experience and wisdom in this area is vital to *coordinate* whole-school success, they cannot shoulder the weight of all things literacy-related.

For a literacy approach to have real impact, it needs to strategically prioritise development of these skills in every subject. Ultimately, we need to pause the teaching conveyer belt and have thoughtful dialogue about how to plan for literacy needs in our individual subject areas. As Geoff Barton implies in the quotation that opens this chapter, it needs to be as clear as possible for novice young people how an expert would approach the literacy demands of our individual subjects. There may be whole-school policies that run alongside this, but the reality is that it needs to be broken down for it to have transferable impact on students' literacy skills. The most obvious place to start is by deconstructing the reading expectations of our subjects.

The Challenges in Reading

For the confident reader, reading is a joyful experience, one that can develop into a habit that lasts a lifetime. Yet, for the novice reader, reading can be a hugely infuriating experience, akin to stumbling around in the dark. This clear distinction forges a gap in reading skills that, as Daniel Rigney (2010) argues, only widens over time. As Rigney states:

> While good readers gain new skills very rapidly, and quickly move from learning to read to reading to learn, poor readers become increasingly frustrated with the act of reading, and try to avoid reading where possible.

Inevitably this leads to a significant and marked gulf in understanding of language and word consciousness. Research by the Department for Education in 2010 showed that at the age of seven this word poverty is already extensive: 'Children in the top quartile have 7100; children in the lowest have 300'. This gap then continues to be forged incrementally, so by the time adult age is reached, as a recent report from the 'Research for the Skills of Life' highlighted:

> 17.8 million adults (56% of the adult working population) in England had literacy skills below GCSE grade C (the equivalent of level 2). Of these, 5.2 million (one in six of the adult population) lacked functional literacy; that is, the level needed to get by in life at work.

If ever there was a statistic to make us stifle our literacy inspired yaw, this is it.

There is also the clear distinction between speaking and reading. Speaking is an innate skill, but according to psychologists such as Stephen Pinker (2015), reading is not. Pinker argues that 'while children are wired for sound, print is an optional accessory that must be painstakingly bolted on'. Reading is not just a written code for speech; it is an entirely new language and process for young people to acquire. Without this capacity to make sense of words and ideas through reading, it is not an understatement to suggest their experience of school is made demonstrably harder. E. D. Hirsch (2013) notes that 'Vocabulary size is a convenient proxy for a whole range of educational attainments and abilities – not just skill in reading, writing, listening, and speaking, but also general knowledge of science, history and the arts'.

Awareness of this is vital for us as educators; it fuels a desire to galvanise and drive a common, whole-school approach to ensure we are teaching both reading and writing more effectively in our subject domains. While there are a range of other factors that will impact this development, we all have a moral purpose to strive to reduce these gaps.

Teaching Reading Skills

So, what do we need to make explicit when teaching reading across our subjects? The first step is to reflect carefully on our curriculum demands. As departments and individual teachers, we need complete clarity on the reading requirements in our various subjects at the different levels. Questions we should be wrestling with include:

1. How much reading is required for our students to achieve well?

2. What is the style and format of reading?

3. Are our students being given plenty of opportunities to practise reading this kind of material?

A Reading Plan

Once we have secured our knowledge of the expectations, we can start to proactively plan out strategies to assist in developing more confident readers. This can be broken down as clearly as possible: what is the audience, purpose and style of words that our students will need to know in our subject? This style of reading then needs to be shared with students and built in regularly to lessons, preventing any shock or lack of understanding that may arise when presented with reading material in an unfamiliar scenario.

Then we need to actively teach reading strategies, going beyond the basics of asking questions after a text to assess understanding. Clearly this will not assist those who struggle most with reading; it is during the process of reading that they find their difficulties. The failure to answer questions will just serve to demotivate them further and reinforce their perception of themselves as poor readers.

As we have seen throughout this book, it is easy for us in our position as experts to have certain expectations about what students are capable of as readers. The reality is that when presented with challenging reading, young people often lack the resilience, or are not equipped with the skills, to be able to pick out information. All too regularly, they completely give up. One of our main aims, in this respect, is to inspire in our students the ability to retain focus, perseverance and commitment to their reading.

Developing Persevering Readers

Daniel Willingham (2017) argues that 'If you're a good reader, you're more likely to enjoy a story because reading it doesn't seem like work'. In order to encourage perseverance from our more reluctant readers we need to tap into some basic motivational premises. The first is what Willingham calls in 'The Reading Mind' a reading 'self-concept': a more positive attitude towards the challenges of reading.

A simple way to help students is to prime them with some background to the issues or concepts explored in the text before they begin reading. This will focus their thinking and allow them to grasp some of the concepts explored in the text before having to grapple with them in print. Then, we might consider releasing a text slowly, pausing to ensure that students are tracking the ideas as they read, or even reading carefully through the text alongside them. This can be done by revealing a specific paragraph or section of the text at a time and following this with discussion to strengthen their understanding.

All too often, we will launch a challenging text at students and watch as they helplessly flounder through the material. By enabling our students to understand how to tackle more challenging texts, they will be encouraged to read both more often and beyond their comfort zones. This needs to be followed by positive affirmation from us, celebrating with them the fact they are adopting a reading mindset.

We can also model comprehension to students, actively talking them through our thought process as we read. Knowledge of our students reading capacity and questioning are vital here, as we increase their performance and ability through checking their understanding. There are three distinct reading strategies to practise with students which will help them to find meaning and clarity in texts. Each should be modelled initially, demonstrating clearly how students can apply the strategy, before their own independent practise is then monitored.

1. Skimming

The first essential reading skill is the ability to skim a text in order to generate an impression of it. Non-fiction texts will make up the majority of reading that students do outside of English class, and skimming is a strategy that can help them to deconstruct meaning. Clearly, they need to know what they are looking through a text for, so spending time considering the nuances of exam questions in relations to texts will help with this strategy. It is then about helping them to identify the key elements that they need to know. To do this well, we need to train students to track the topic sentences or paragraphs, and discern if the information is useful or not. We can coach them to skim material to check for key words that might arise, particularly in terms of the words that make up a question. All this helps in building students' confidence in reading and responding to texts quickly.

2. Scanning

Scanning requires more deliberate and discerning reading, as students will be searching for relevant information. Giving students a text to read and words to identify, then using a timer to ensure that they have to quickly scan and pick out key words, can develop confidence in this strategy. This can be turned into a race, further building up students' ability to quickly pick out information from a text. Scanning is a particularly helpful approach if students need to decode texts quickly in an exam situation.

3. Summarising

Summarising the content of texts can be useful in all subjects and improves students' ability to identify the important aspects of a text. Asking students to summarise what they have read in their own words will help them to identify exactly what the text is about. Immediately after reading, they can write a fifty-word summary in (as far as possible) their own words about what they have read. This requires them to mentally track the content of a text chronologically, then summarise what they feel is the essential information. It also helps teachers to pick up any misconceptions in their reading and guide their understanding when we take feedback from them.

Vocabulary Deficiencies

It is very simple: if students do not understand a certain amount of the words they are reading, they will not be able to follow a text. When the range of challenging words in a text increases, it becomes more frustrating and demotivating for reluctant readers. Explicit teaching of vocabulary is therefore vital across the subject spectrum, to prepare young people with the skills to approach challenging vocabulary. In our lessons there is much value in building up more of an inquisitive, word-conscientious environment; to tap into the excitement that young people feel when they can successfully use a new word in a new context.

First, we have to be clear on what Isabel L. Beck *et al* (2013) describe as 'Tier Three' words, which 'tend to be limited to specific domains'. Coming up with a list of subject-specific words as a collaborative departmental process means we are all clear about the identified words that we need to actively teach our students and build their familiarity with. These are the words that could appear in examinations and have the potential to throw our students off completely.

It is then important to teach and repeat new words actively within our lessons. This is where the dictionary can be more of a hindrance than a help. Often, the dictionary can confuse students with oblique definitions (after they have spent what feels like an eternity searching for the word in the first place), that then need to be clarified by us. A far better use of lesson time is to come up with our own student-friendly definition of a word, which will give them the best possible start in grappling with meaning. There needs to be frequent opportunities for students to practise this new word, in both their writing and in their speech. Repetition and repeated exposure is also vital in securing understanding of more complex vocabulary; students will need to return to the words and practise using them in a variety of contexts.

Modelling our own enthusiasm for the mystery of words is also infectious. One way to do this is by taking students on a journey through the etymology of words, exploring where certain words originate from. This is an adventure that teachers in every subject can undertake – who knew that trigonometry was first used in 1610 and spawned from the Greek trigonon (triangle) and gonia (angle)? As Andy Tharby (2017) makes clear in his book *Making Every English Lesson Count*, people 'are far more likely to remember a word's meaning when it comes complete with a postage-stamped size biography'.

Inspiring a Reading Culture

When we talk of the lofty aim of inspiring a reading culture in our schools, our focus is on cementing a reading habit with young people. A habit very quickly becomes a passion, something that we feel we cannot live without.

It is, however, challenging to develop this habit in adolescence, often the point at which reading is most neglected. As the son of an English teacher and a primary school teacher, both literature graduates, my house growing up was steeped in reading. Yet, still, my reading habit rapidly declined in my adolescence (I blame a slightly unhealthy obsession with Oasis), only to return in my late teens. So, how can we sustain a habit that is often cultivated and formed in early childhood?

Role Modelling

Part of inspiring teenagers to read is not to underestimate the influence our own modelling and love for reading can have, regardless of what subject we teach. Taking opportunities to pause and share what we are reading with students is hugely powerful. When I completed the '52 books in a year' reading challenge, inspired by Andy Miller's *The Year of Reading Dangerously*, I used part of an online blog to share the journey with my students, giving me the excuse to rant and rave about all the reading I was enjoying. It had the unintended effect of encouraging some of my students to set their own reading challenges; a positive way to take the first steps in forging a reading habit. Our modelling of intellectual curiosity, and the discussion of the various worlds that reading can open up, will help our students to experiment more with their own reading.

Reading Conversations

How often do we spend time talking to students about what they are reading and talking the time to recommend books? It is a powerful moment when a teacher suggests a book to a student, with the potential impact of transforming their relationship. The more frequently this happens in schools, the more widespread and ubiquitous reading conversations will become.

Whole-School Agendas

The more varied and interesting activities that can be set up to inspire young readers throughout school, the better. The 'Drop Everything and Read' initiative has been successful in a range of schools. Bringing the fun and joy into reading is also evident in 'Caught Reading' tasks, with staff and students engaging in entertaining pictures that demonstrate them reading. Reading groups can filter through every year group – all building further the sense of a reading community. 'Reading Champions' can also be a way to motivate and encourage young people to read more, with rewards and recognition given to students who are driving reading forward.

Librarians

As the beating heart of reading in a school, the library is vital, providing accessibility and motivation for young people. A knowledgeable and inspirational librarian can make such a difference in encouraging students to read. I have been fortunate to work with excellent librarians whose passion, love and enthusiasm for reading is is palpable. It is important that students make active choices about what they read, but those choices can be guided in the hands of an expert.

Writing

In each of our subjects the writing demands will vary significantly. Throughout the school day students have to adapt to a range of unique and nuanced written styles. Ensuring that they have a clear and distinct understanding of how to write for their different classes will assist them in varying between them. There are the obvious conventions that we should encourage them to consider and some important questions, such as:

1. What is the purpose of the piece of writing?

2. How will the writing be structured?

3. What will the tone of the writing be: formal or informal?

4. What vocabulary is required to complete the task well?

5. Who is the intended audience for the piece of writing?

As we have seen already, the act of modelling is vital in securing students' understanding about the style of writing that they should be aiming to replicate. Again, it is important that we instruct students to slow down and plan out their writing; encouraging consideration of exactly what the aims of the task are and helping them develop a vision for their writing is crucial.

Connectives are the bedrock of writing in a number of subjects, building clarity and direction in students' writing. Sharing the connectives that they might use to structure their answer will help them to direct and sustain the appropriate formality. One way to improve the planning aspect and accuracy of writing is to give our students scope and time for oral rehearsal. This could be something that they do individually or in pairs to help them decide how they will approach a task before putting pen to paper. At this point, we can listen in and give our input to prevent any misconceptions. It is also a confidence builder for the students: once they have spoken about their writing, they can then get it down on paper.

The process of building students' confidence in writing in different subjects requires careful revision and editing. While our concise feedback will guide them on the areas they need to work on, the re-drafting process discussed earlier will also help students to understand exactly how to improve their writing in a particular style. Fundamentally, the art of developing confidence in a writing style requires extensive practice. There needs to be time allocated weekly for students to practise writing in the style demanded of them by our subjects.

English blogger and Head of English, Chris Curtis, developed a strategy whereby all of the teachers in his department complete similar writing tasks with their students every Friday. Students know that every Friday they will complete one of the engaging two-hundred word challenges. As he states in his excellent blog: 'Their books are full of writing. Lots of writing. Their books also tell a story. They tell the story of how they are getting better' (Curtis, 2017). Not only does this approach avoid a department replicating planning time and improve staff wellbeing, but the regular practise of writing develops the resilience and motivation of students.

Spelling

Young people lose copious marks across all subjects when they reach examination levels by not being able to spell subject-specific words. Developing confident spelling is a crucial, lifelong skill, far beyond the narrow constraints of exam specifications. Again, a common, whole-school approach is necessary; spelling cannot just be 'solved' by English teachers. The more students work on this area of their writing and the more it is encouraged by staff across the school, the more spelling standards will improve.

Spelling needs to be a 'live' point during lessons. Encouraging students to grow in confidence by verbally spelling and sounding out words will result in these being used in writing with improved accuracy. Spelling also needs to be a focus across all subjects in the written feedback we give to students. Marking a spelling mistake in a students' workbook is utterly superfluous; they need to take the time to learn that particular word, before writing out corrections and then being tested.

Marking with a literacy lens is simple and time effective; all we need to do is highlight an area for our students to return to. This ensures the onus is on them and they must invest the time thinking about how to address the area of concern. The importance of proofreading becomes clear; asking students to carefully check over their work so that they take ownership of it will result in greater attention to detail. Distributing a list of some common grammatical spelling errors to look out for will help them to pick up their errors.

Then, we need to attempt to demystify the complexity of spelling for students:

1. **Mention and identify patterns:** While the English language is remarkably frustrating in its sporadic use of patterns, looking at the morphology of words (how they are formed and their relationship to other words) will help students to remember them. This could involve examining letter patterns and common groups of words with students. This will help them to remember common spelling rules.

2. **Interleave testing:** The earlier chapter on memory highlighted the importance of low-stakes quizzing. It may be that we test students on a collection of spellings at the start of the week, then repeat the same test later to strengthen their understanding. Then in later tests we build in words that students found difficult to ensure that they are confident with spelling them. My eight-year-old nephew gets a list of ten words to learn for homework every week. While he (usually!) dutifully learns his words each week, he is never asked to return to them in subsequent weeks. When he is tested on those words much later, he has forgotten them again. Interleaving the words that we are asking students to learn will help them to retain these words for longer.

3. **Teach spelling through content:** Using the content of lessons to focus on key spellings is vital. This could be done through the reading that we use in lessons, pausing to make sure that students know exactly how to spell particular words.

4. **Practise in writing:** Once students have learned how to spell a word they should then be expected to implement it in their writing repeatedly. This will reinforce their confidence and increase the chances of them being able to spell it later.

We arrive in the teaching profession deeply steeped in idealism: we want to make an impact and transform our students' lives. Unremitting high expectations about the standards of writing and reading does begin to make the mark we still sometimes allow ourselves to dream of. It will set up the students we teach with the best possible opportunities for success in life.

Slow Questions

1. Do you know the literacy demands of your individual subject(s)?

2. How much and how often do you ask students to read in your subject(s)?

3. Do you coach students on how to approach the style of reading required?

4. How often do you model and discuss your own reading habits with students?

5. Are you driving forward reading with your students, encouraging and providing them with guidance on reading for pleasure?

6. Do you make spelling a focus in your lessons?

7. Do you deconstruct spelling and use a range of strategies?

8. Are you literacy aware in your marking? Do you mark for grammar and spelling alongside content? Do you encourage students to proofread with a literacy lens?

CHAPTER 15: TEACHING THE SECRETS OF EFFECTIVE REVISION

Half of my life is an act of revision.
John Irving

It is a statement that never fails to fill teachers with frustration and despair, usually arriving with worrying proximity to an assessment or examination: 'To be honest Sir, I'm not really too sure how to revise'. The confession is always whispered in a slightly embarrassed way, as if our innocent student knows that, at this stage in their school career, they should be armed with the ability to revise independently.

Then there is the even more infuriating line – 'I don't need to revise!' – the spectacular dose of over-confidence that gives superhuman powers to some students in the face of exams. There may be not a single strand of evidence that would support their claims, but still they blindly march on, absolving themselves of all responsibility for revision.

The Wilderness of Revision

Both responses are maddening because teachers are, of course, very aware that effective revision is vital for students to do to achieve their full potential. We have done everything we possibly can in our teaching: low-stakes testing, regular interleaving of material, extensive student practice and hours of painstaking feedback have all been gainfully employed in our carefully constructed plan for their success. Yet, when it matters most, we become irrelevant and they are utterly on their own, let loose into the wilderness of revision. There may have been endless material that we have laden them with, but what they do, or don't do, with them is entirely at their discretion.

It is easy for students to take the wrong direction, to stumble across monumental glaciers, to collapse and give up completely in these individual endeavours. In their desire to do well, there are a minefield of different approaches and techniques that students may well attempt. Type 'revision strategies' into that close friend of adolescents, Google, and around 700,000 search results come up. There is a maze of conflicting ways to approach using their time for revision, all loudly exclaiming their merit ('the secret to exam success' or 'the best way to revise') to impressionable young people.

Ideally, our role is to arm students with strategies that will help them to avoid such panic searching and become a more direct, simplified and informed master of revision strategies. Our professional obligation is to sift through this maze of advice so that we can confidently coach, cajole and guide them. To stretch the metaphor to breaking point: we can't let students disappear into the wilderness of revision without our expert advice.

The Revision Traps

Imagine the following scenario: David has been revising geography for two hours. The bulk of his time has been spent re-reading his notes and highlighting what he feels are essential pieces of information. After two hours he pats himself on the back, yawns and eagerly takes a well-earned *Call of Duty* PlayStation break. During the next thirty minutes of cathartic violence, does David reflect on the efficiency of what he has done in the previous two hours? Does he question whether or not he has meaningfully learned any information? Does he quiz himself on the knowledge that he believes he has secured? Or, does he fall straight into the obvious trap: because he is now familiar with the information, does he think that he knows it?

We may be being rather harsh on young David here; he is trying, after all! Perhaps it is, in fact, a vital skill we need our students to engage with: reflecting on how well they are revising. Daniel Willingham (2009) argues that 'students typically know little about how their memories work and, as a result, do not know how to study effectively'.

In reality, even as adults, we often fail to slow down in our busy lives in order to check if we have really processed the range of information we may have come across throughout the day. The growing popularity of online activity means we are absorbing and reading more and more content. Of course, while there are significant positives associated with using the internet, its presence often results in much more skim reading, without us really taking the time to understand and engage with what we have read.

Another facet of human nature is that we have the tendency to take the easier path when trying to learn and study. Peter C. Brown *et al* (2014) note that 'when the going is harder and slower it doesn't feel productive, we are drawn to strategies that feel more fruitful, unaware that the gains from these strategies are often temporary'. Guiding students to avoid the following unproductive strategies will help them to make better decisions about how to use their time.

Cramming

Having pulled off the ambivalent approach in the weeks leading up to an exam, a great number of students will be haunted by feelings of last-minute panic. They will then set off on a binge revision marathon, and the night before the exam they will stay up until all hours to revise. Last-minute, single-minded cramming has some immediate benefits: there will be an immediate 'knowledge' high which can then be replicated in the exam. Yet, as we have seen, it will very soon be forgotten. The immediate knowledge comedown happens quickly and leaves us sluggish, like a rapid decrease in blood sugar. My dogged, fear-driven cramming for my biology higher examination did manage to scrape me a pass. Yet, if you asked me now, I would struggle to give a very simple definition of 'photosynthesis'; this shallow knowledge has completely disappeared.

While there may be immediate benefits of cramming, one of the issues with its practice lies in the intense anxiety and stress it can evoke. Manic cramming before an exam almost guarantees a dreadful night's sleep, as adrenaline and stress will be flying around the body. Sleep is integral in the formation of enduring memories. We are all familiar with that haze and lack of clarity we feel as a result of a poor night's sleep. It also heightens our emotional reactions, and stress becomes much more of a forceful enemy without sleep. By not tackling cramming habits we may inadvertently be allowing students to march, zombie-style and stressed out, into an exam hall.

Re-reading and Highlighting

There is one activity that dominates revision: re-reading. We have all fallen prey to its seductive allure, poring over notes and textbooks in the vain attempt to magically absorb (photosynthesis-like) the information. Its origins are a mystery, yet it is what we have done for generations and it is the advice most frequently offered by teachers: 'read carefully over your notes'.

Perhaps even more tantalising is to couple this re-reading with the humble highlighter. Come revision time the highlighter is in significant demand, waved around with its full potential exhausted. Many a student will present us with a beautifully highlighted page, then frown in concern when we ask them why they have highlighted information and what the significance of it is. After all, it does feel rather delightful to make something fluorescent, but trying to retain it is much more challenging.

There is a simple strategy to explore the efficacy of a highlighter ourselves: read through a piece of work highlighting key information, turn the page over and complete a self-quiz. What information can we remember? This busy and quick activity feeds the overconfidence we have already explored; highlighting and re-reading are often used by students to reassure themselves that they are adequately prepared. To return to *Make it Stick*:

> Re-reading has three strikes against it. It is time consuming. It doesn't result in durable learning. And it often involves a kind of unwitting self-deception, as growing familiarity with the text comes to feel like mastery of the content (Brown *et al*, 2014).

Explaining to students why re-reading may not be the best strategy, and instead giving them clear direction and training on how they could better use their time, may save them many fruitless hours.

Tackling Revision Procrastination

Even the most conscientious and focused among us are motivated by short-term and immediate rewards. For adolescents the short-term rewards, as we have already seen, are extensive and remarkably loud. Why grapple with simultaneous equations when the instant gratification of a Snapchat message awaits us? Revision is challenging enough in a utopian environment, such as a quiet home context that is free of distractions. For many young people this ideal is impossible; their home environment is packed full of distractions.

As teachers, we can acknowledge these revision blocks with students and do our best to encourage them to take proactive steps to address them. Here is a nifty 'top-five tips to avoid procrastination' to share with students, with the ingenious mnemonic (a tool, as we have seen, of splendid memory power) of 'STUDY'.

1. **S**witch your phone off

2. **T**ake breaks

3. **U**se a list or plan

4. **D**on't use the internet

5. **Y**es or no: test.

The phone and the internet are the most obvious procrastination devils (I know they haunted me while writing this book!) Young people need guidance to avoid these distractions, with even the sight of a phone reducing a person's ability to focus. The best approach is to remove both: the phone and internet need to be left in a different room.

The ability to manage themselves and their time (self-efficacy) is another key point to explore with students; if they believe they can focus and concentrate on the task ahead, they will have more chance of persevering. Encouraging students to avoid music and work in quiet focus will help them to use their time well and efficiently.

To do this, we can shatter the myth of multi-tasking, explaining to them that they will be more successful if they focus on exploring one thing at a time. A colleague of mine uses the example of attempting to drive while speaking on a mobile phone to demonstrate how this shatters focus and concentration (hence it being extremely hazardous and illegal!) The same is true with revision and multi-tasking: it switches the brain's attentional system and removes focus. Dave Crenshaw (2008) exposes this in *The Myth of Multitasking*, arguing that multi-tasking is impossible and should be renamed 'switch-tasking'.

Factoring in study breaks to their revision schedules will assist our students to avoid the lure of procrastination. The Pomodoro Technique (2009) is another useful strategy to coach young people on how to manage their time. This involves using a timer to ensure that they work steadily for fifty-five minutes, then allow themselves time out for a five-minute break to do as they please. This ensures focus for the majority of the hour and avoids switching between revision and other tasks. It also allows students to take time to check in on the world that is calling for them so persuasively, before returning to the single-minded focus required of revision.

Tackling Learning Styles

A common revision practice is for young people to cater to what has been defined by their 'learning style'. Learning styles offer a claim about how we best learn; be it visual, audio, kinaesthetic or a whole host of other labels. The idea is that we learn best when the mode of presentation matches the style in which we learn. Students' learning styles are conventionally identified through a self-questionnaire (perhaps where the first warning signs may appear).

Issues with learning styles are, again, clear. Graham Nuthall (2007) argues that there has been no real evidence presented to date to prove the validity of learning styles. His apt summary is that they 'are about motivation and management, they are not about learning'. In The Sutton Trust's report 'What makes great teaching?' (2014) the authors also identified that learning styles have no impact on learner achievement. There has been little meaningful research that can justify a positive impact they have on young people.

More importantly, the message delivered as a result of learning styles can be hugely limiting and destructive for students. It feeds a defeatist narrative: I am not that kind of learner, therefore I will be no good at this. The same could perhaps be argued of any case of a child being labelled (be it high ability, lower ability), it means that they identify this as part of their capacity to learn. For the student revising, it means the temptation is to avoid challenging thinking, and do only what they feel fits with their learning style. If they have been identified as a 'visual learners', they will then seek to hide and take comfort in the sanctuary of 'visual learning'.

So, how do we encourage students to see beyond the myths they might have been fed about learning in the past? Our repeated motto should be that revision should be effortful, active and sustained. As far back as 1890, William James (2017) argued that 'a curious peculiarity of our memory is that things are impressed better by active than by passive repetition'. Tapping into strategies that will maximise this 'curious peculiarity' will help our students to confidently prepare for their examinations.

The Revision Tool Kit

Parental Support

The more we can engage and unite with parents in our mission to scaffold students' revision, the more chance they will be supported effectively at home. This requires informing them early on about the examinations their child will face, and the best mechanisms they can use to revise for our subject. Often, parents can feel isolated from the stress their teenagers might be going through. By proactively engaging with them, they will begin to feel like a valued part of the process. Sharing research on how their child should go about revising and providing practical tips can also ensure that they join the mission to help their children use their time more effectively.

Timetable

The first thing we need to do is assist students in the process of developing a practical and useful revision timetable. There are a number of traps students fall into when deciding what to revise. They may invest substantially more time in their favourite subjects; they may revise what they perceive themselves as being 'good at'; or, they may completely neglect their stronger subjects. What we can do to help is encourage them to plan out their revision so as to ensure that there is a comprehensive coverage of all their subjects.

Simplifying the process for them and making it realistic will help alleviate feelings of stress and anxiety. A rigid or demanding timetable could have the impact of putting students off doing any work, while the converse will mean that they don't do enough! First, they need to consider how long they have before the exams and the amount of units they need to cover. This could generate a tick list of key course elements that need to be revised, which can be checked off when they are covered. Then they should plan for regular and active concentrated shots of revision, not sitting revising for hours at a time.

To enable this to happen we must ensure they start this process early in the year. In this plan, it is important that students allow for study breaks which are a vital part of the process. Fresh air and a short walk can do wonders for being able to return and focus. The key thing to guide on is perspective: students need to be reminded that this is an important part of their life and some sacrifices are required.

Self-Testing

We have clarified that the skimming of class notes is not going to assist in securing knowledge. Instead, what will be more useful in retaining knowledge is going through the process of self-testing. This can be achieved by following the following strategies.

Concept mapping: Students should put away all their notes and instead make a concept note, highlighting all of the information they have on a particular topic. They may feel they have all the knowledge they need, but this approach forces them to recall and process the material that they have gone through. This process is circular, as they can return to their notes and check what they might have missed, thus filling in the gaps in their knowledge. The construction of a mind map is also helpful, although for it to be useful it needs to live up to its name and become a literal map of the mind's eye, with the information learned and absorbed completely. This might require practice and repeating the mind map again in different ways. Students completing their own knowledge organisers (the vital information they need to know in a particular unit of work) is also a helpful way to use their time, particularly if they can then compare it with the original organiser that they may have from the start of the unit.

Spaced testing: Having invested time in reading over material and seeking to understand it, the immediacy of a self-written test or the input of someone else testing on content can be very help. Even better, however, is to wait an hour, revise something else, then come back and complete a test on the previous work. This will ensure that students must think hard to recall the information; a true test if they can replicate it in exam conditions. Then they can then return to reflect on areas they haven't yet mastered.

Test exam questions: The most obvious technique to encourage students to use when revising is to complete an exam-style question. To mirror the conditions completely, this should be done in the atmosphere that reflects an exam: in silence and with the amount of time they will have in the exam. To generate real 'test-wiseness', trying to make sure they complete a practice question on the range of topics that might come up in the exam will help them feel more authentically and justifiably confident.

What will make this even more helpful is if they receive feedback on it, so as to guide them on what they need to do more of. If students can be provided with a bank of exemplar answers to compare their own responses to, this will help them to self-assess and develop a further understanding of their own knowledge. Providing students with different examples and asking them to compare and contrast them for efficacy can also help in securing knowledge.

An important element of revision is establishing an open dialogue with students, and encouraging them to send us examples of questions they have completed, or to seek us out for further dialogue. Clearly, at times, this may not be possible; in this case, there are a wealth of online alternatives that can support revision for our subjects.

Flashcards

Flashcards can be a splendid means for students to engage with content and condense information down to cues. The process of making the flashcards themselves is a useful practice: involving the dilution of key notes and ideas onto card. This requires the active recall of information, as you seek to process concepts and information you have learned in your own words and in a condensed fashion.

Flashcards can also be used in different environments and places, allowing them to be a mobile form of revision that requires self-reflection. For them to be effective they need to involve testing, using them to test their own knowledge or have someone help them. The art of writing flashcards by hand will also help to reject the call of internet and other electronic devices, meaning focus and concentration are essential! Sticky notes can be an even more simplified version of flashcards; placing them at a visual point in their own homes means they will be frequently referred to and help to ensure retention.

Repetition

Repeating information is one of the simplest ways of securing it in our minds. It is effortful and avoids the process of merely reading something over. For repetition to work, however, it needs to go beyond the mechanical and engage with meaning: why is it that the repeated information is true or valid? By encouraging students to actively repeat material, we also encourage them to overlearn and go beyond mastering a topic. They will often underestimate how quickly they will forget a concept or an idea; by repeating it and overlearning it, we can reduce the likelihood of this happening.

The spaced repetition of a test is an excellent means to secure retention, and will help to create stronger memories. Testing after information has been initially learned can check understanding; this should be followed by the same test the next day, then the same test a week later. Going through this repetition will increase the speed at which students can recall information, meaning that they can replicate it quickly in exam situations.

Paired Revision

The sight of our students heading off to revise together can evoke dread: just how much work are they really going to get done? Yet their unity may in fact be a blessing in disguise, for the act of teaching each other can be a very useful revision tool. To return to our philosophical chum Seneca (2003): 'while we teach, we learn'. It is, of course, true in our command of our own subjects: how much more informed and confident are we about our own subjects after having taught them for a number of years? Scientists have dubbed this 'The protégé effect' (2009) – the positive impact that occurs when students explain and teach each other elements of their revision. It is a perfect way to enable active testing, with students testing each other and having immediate access to the correct answer. All this helps revision to be motivational and, dare I say it, introduces an element of fun for young people. Encouraging them to break up long days of revision by working with someone else can be very helpful.

Eat and Sleep Well

Revision for many students is coupled with every sugary treat you can imagine; a mountainous supply that is deemed essential to get them through the process of revising. The problem with this is clear: sugary slumps and caffeine-induced lows result in decreased concentration and less retention of knowledge. While it will not win us any popularity contests, we can encourage students to balance their diet and get enough sleep. We shall arm ourselves with some sleep wisdom in Chapter 19.

The next student who utters 'I don't know how to revise' may well want to find themselves a comfortable chair, as we launch into our widespread, research-informed repertoire of effective revision strategies. By sharing our guidance with them and simplifying the process, we are setting them up for some successful and impactful revision and improved results.

Now that we have done everything in our power to slowly provide our students with the very best opportunities as learners, it is about time we put our own lives under the slow microscope. What better place to start than our relationship with our profession, and our ability to continue to grow and develop as teachers.

Slow Questions

1. Are your students suffering from a lack of clarity about how to revise?

2. Are you tackling the symptoms of over-confident students?

3. Are your students clear on the dangers of cramming?

4. What are the procrastination avoidance tips you can arm your students with?

5. Can you help your students to construct a revision timetable?

6. What self-testing techniques do you want students to employ in their revision?

PART V: SLOW TEACHER IMPROVEMENT

CHAPTER 16:
REFLECT AND REFINE:
DEVELOPING PASSIONATE
TEACHERS

If we create a culture where every teacher believes they need to improve, not because they are not good enough, but because we can be even better, there is no limit to what we can achieve.
Dylan Wiliam

What keeps us energised, motivated and enthusiastic in our classrooms? When faced with a new academic year, what inspires us to become better versions of ourselves for our students? At the heart of such questions lies our intrinsic motivation: our ability to find joy and purpose in what we do. Managing to sustain this can be utterly transformative in the classroom, with our energy and passion translating into improved student engagement and, ultimately, achievement. It also means we embrace a mindset for ourselves as professionals that is focused on the 'continuous' in 'continuous professional development' (CPD): an inquisitive and optimistic desire to improve.

Teacher Stagnation

In our first few years working in teaching there is a significant drive towards engendering improvement. We receive extensive feedback, we are encouraged to read, reflect and write about our practice, and we watch a huge amount of teaching. Our attitude is also important; we are a metaphorical sponge, keen to learn and become the best teacher we can be. Yet, after the NQT year, there is a palpable drop in this structured guidance and, depending on the quality of the school, we are often left to our own devices. While this autonomy is important and liberating, inevitably there is less investment in reflecting on how effectively we are developing as teachers.

In their research on teacher quality, Eric A. Hanushek and Steven G. Rivkin (2006) suggest that teachers can often stop improving after three years:

> There appear to be important gains in teaching quality in the first year of experience and smaller gains over the next few career years. However, there is little evidence that improvements continue after the first three years.

There is much that can influence this improvement inertia: both the culture of a school and the quality of, and time afforded to, CPD will be, in part, determining factors. An element of lethargy can also seep in when we have taught for a long time and given so much to the role. We find ourselves so busy with the range of demands imposed on us, that we lose the motivation and desire to build on our knowledge base. Teaching the same content and the same syllabus over and over again inevitably feeds this treadmill thinking and a risk-adverse attitude that places up the shutters in the face of change.

Ultimately, it is our own view of teaching and our ability to improve that will have the most transformative difference in moving beyond the three-year road blocks. There is no easy fix; instead, we need to go on a slow, deliberate path of small steps that will help to improve and energise our teaching. Doing so will help us to reconnect with the initial adrenaline that teaching provided, as we become more reflective and more prone to experimenting again.

Potential not Perfection

There are a dizzying range of skills and elements that influence how effective we are in the classroom. Teaching, as we have seen in the examination of its many layers, is a complex and multi-faceted art. The sheer magnitude of the skills required is perfectly, if not rather intimidatingly, captured by Lee Shulman (2004) in *The Wisdom of Practice*:

> After 30 years of doing such work, I have concluded that classroom teaching is perhaps the most complex, most challenging, and most demanding, subtle, nuanced, and frightening activity that our species has ever invented. The only time a physician could possibly encounter a situation of comparable complexity would be in the emergency room of a hospital during or after a natural disaster.

What may be seen as (hugely!) daunting can in fact be liberating, with this proving to be yet another example of the varied and exciting nature of teaching as a profession. The scope of detail and learning we can go through also means we can effectively never attain the lofty goal of teaching perfection. Shulman's philosophy begins to remove the stress and competitive element of teaching and makes the goal of teaching simple: we should all be on a path to becoming one step better than we were before. One way to achieve this is to open up our classroom doors to others.

Observations

'Observation' has the potential to set stress cortisones flying for teachers, evoking the arbitrary judgement of a one-off performance management summation of our teaching. Inevitably, given the high stakes pressure, such experiences do not allow us to perform at our best or provide the conditions for us to actively take on feedback. Often, an observation focussed culture leads to a furtive teaching existence, where we hide ourselves away for the majority of the year, receiving little feedback. This insular approach leaves us frustrated, as we repeat our mistakes, and without any clarity about how much more effective we could be. It also, inevitably, leads to high teaching staff turnover: why would we stay in an environment that does not fuel an open desire for improvement? John Tomsett (2015) explores this lack of openness in *This Much I Know about Love Over Fear*, suggesting that 'the one thing that destroys the energy of a workplace culture is a climate of fear'.

Removing grades from lesson observations, a thankfully much more widespread practice, is a positive step in the right direction. It ensures that the focus returns to what is actually happening in the classroom, rather than hearing a grade then blindly moving on. The more we are open and transparent about what is happening in our classrooms and actively seek feedback, the less stress we experience about having people watch us. Importantly, it also means we are more likely to present an authentic vision of our daily practice, not striving to meet whatever subjective checklist is fashionable to generate a judgement on us. Instead, we can start to use observations as a collaborative approach to improve our teaching.

Observations from peers or others can provide us with concrete, specific and individual guidance about the marginal changes that could have a huge impact on our teaching. It also frees us up to take risks in the classroom, to experiment with different strategies and to receive feedback on those new and energising endeavours. Instead of the climate of fear, we prioritise our discussions about what we are also passionate about: our subjects and how to teach them effectively.

One way to do this is to identify an aspect of our practice that we want to improve, and then ask a colleague to observe a short section of our lesson in which this is the focus. This encourages us to objectively assess our teaching practice and reflect on what we think we should prioritise in our development. It also vital in encouraging the best teaching practices to be shared across the school, and in helping to create an environment where professional conversations about teaching dominate. This philosophy of continuous feedback is embraced by Michaela School:

> Every day at Michaela, teachers watch their colleagues teach – five minutes, ten minutes, thirty minutes perhaps. Teachers receive feedback on their practice from every member of staff – teaching fellows, Heads of Department, SLE and admin staff will chip in what they notice. Every teacher will watch and be watched hundreds of times in a year. No grades, no top-down feedback, just teachers, trying to get better at teaching, by looking, learning and receiving extensive feedback (Birbalsingh, 2016).

Modelling

An alternative, and equally worthwhile approach, is to ask a colleague if you could watch a section of their lesson and look at how they approach a particular element of teaching. Watching another teacher is without doubt one of the most energising things we can do; it motivates and inspires us and guides us on different approaches. It reminds us of the core purpose of schools and how we are all powerfully engaged in this mission. It is even more helpful when the observation can be combined with another individual who can assist in pointing out the subtleties and nuances of the teaching that we might miss.

In reality, a huge amount of our teacher persona is an amalgamation of the qualities we have viewed in others. It might be inspiring teachers who have taught us, or those we have observed who have given us a jolt of energy about the possibilities of what our students can achieve in the classroom. We adopt numerous strategies from these individuals, either consciously or unconsciously, and combine our own stamp of character on them. Continuing to build in what we see in others is one way in which we can evolve and improve in our classrooms.

Cross-curricular Observations

Taking the time to open our doors and step into practice that may be beyond our immediate department also allows us to consider learning from a new perspective. It reminds us about the challenges of learning as we piece together how the teacher is approaching a skill.

Watching a lesson outside of our subject area also removes our subject-knowledge fixation; inevitably, when we observe colleagues in our own department, we are considering how they are approaching the subject. We also start to become more nuanced about what we are observing, and this opens up new perspectives about teaching. Again, it illuminates those 'bright spots' that Chip and Dan Heath (2011) highlight in *Switch*: the pockets of inspirational teaching that exist in every school and would otherwise remain hidden.

Dialogue

Schools can become draining when we realise how little time is spent discussing the core business: teaching and learning in our classrooms. Data, admin and workload issues can begin to take over and leave us feeling lacklustre and overwhelmed. We can fall into the time trap that has haunted us throughout this book: adopting the defeatist and ubiquitous narrative that says we don't have time to speak about teaching.

Instead, being proactive in forging teaching and learning conversations will help to focus us on what we are invested in spending hours on daily. In every school there will be a small army of teachers who are hugely passionate about teaching and learning; however, there needs to be the mechanisms in place to bring these individuals together. Shaun Allison and Andy Tharby (2015) suggest that:

> ...all great schools have something in common. They are filled to the brim with enthusiastic teachers who enjoy talking about teaching, sharing ideas and finding things out. Similarly they will have leaders who facilitate and encourage this.

The use of initiative and a clear mission is needed to unite these teachers. Many schools now use groups who meet regularly to discuss educational books and research, or teaching and learning teams who are responsible for driving the agenda for teaching across the school. A colleague and I have set up a 'Teacher Advocates' group in our school to bring together a range of voices who are passionate about spending time discussing teaching. Each department in the school has their own 'Advocate' who is responsible for passing on the findings of the sessions to their departments. Any mechanism that allows for regular meetings to share thinking about how to develop and improve aspects of teaching can plant the seeds of change that could quickly disperse around a school.

Taking these steps doesn't require a revolution in our schools, or for us to take the lead on new agendas. On an individual basis, the more we seek out collaborative learning conversations about how best to approach a topic or how best to hone a particular skill, the more we learn and develop from those around us. Such conversations fill us with optimism and hope about what we might be able to achieve in our classrooms. An even better approach is if we can begin to develop a more structured and consistent basis to these conversations by finding a coach.

Coaching

Paul Bambrick-Santoyo (2012) notes that 'teachers are like tennis players – they develop most quickly when they receive frequent feedback and opportunities to practice'. Finding an individual who can perform the role of a supportive coach can supercharge our development as teachers.

There is a clear distinction between mentoring and coaching. Any mentoring relationship is based on more informed knowledge or experience, which has at its heart a focus on guiding and instructing another individual. Coaching, on the other hand, is a structured process of learning between a coach and a coachee, which is much more about a relationship of equality. In a coaching relationship there is no element of judgement; it is designed to be developmental and non-judgemental and therefore needs to be distinct from performance management. Indeed, its sole purpose is to unlock the potential of an individual.

It is also important that the dialogue has elements of challenge and probing in order to assist in creating change and growth. With the principle of coaching being a positive relationship, this feedback is much more likely to result in improvements. To return to John Tomsett's (2015) idea about fear restricting improvement, coaching can make those conversations easier and more productive.

Coaching Models

For coaching to be effective it needs a sense of clarity and purpose; otherwise time can be lost without having any impact on teaching practice. Andy Buck (2017) uses the incremental coaching strategy, stating that:

> [Coaching] typically involves a short drop-in to a lesson where the short coaching conversations that follows, ideally that day, elicits the areas of strength and a single area of focus for improvement with some strategies to try.

Teachers then have a week to work on that particular aspect before a return visit. The popular GROW model is also useful to ensure that coaching sessions are strategic, with this providing a framework for conversation.

Goal: setting aims for the session as well as for the long term.

Reality: checking to explore the current situation.

Options: and alternative strategies or courses of action.

What: is to be done, when, by whom and the will to do it.

The purpose of this is to ensure that the individual being coached is objective in exploring the problem, while the coach acts as a facilitator in assisting them to see the 'blind spots' of their problem. Coaching, when it becomes a part of a school's culture, can have a hugely positive impact on both classroom teaching and staff wellbeing. It requires training, patience and time in order to ensure that it can progressively make a difference.

Reflection

While dialogue, coaching and observations are vital in opening different perspectives and viewpoints about how to approach teaching, there is more than a grain of truth in the famous William Henley poem 'Invictus' (2015): 'I am the captain of my fate/ I am the master of my soul'. What will have a defining influence on giving us control over improvements to our teaching practice is the capacity to reflect and refine what we are doing in the classroom. After all, for the great majority of the school day and week, we find ourselves alone in our classrooms. If we can use this time to learn lessons as we teach, then we learn to be more self-critical and become agents of our own improvement.

Reflection is one means to slow ourselves down and step outside of the repetitive and draining loop of a busy teaching timetable. There is also the reality of how difficult it is to develop an understanding about an aspect of our practice, without investing the time in trying to dilute and crystallise our thinking. To the philosopher Socrates 'the unexamined life is not worth living'. Without a process of reflection and ownership over what we are doing, we are reduced, again, to a cog in a wheel. Embracing change, however, requires discipline, openness and a clear plan.

Find a Format

Finding a way to reflect that works on an individual level is a worthwhile process that may help reflection become more of a habit. The growing popularity of online blogs highlights how useful this medium can be for developing reflective qualities. There are a range of benefits to blogging: it forges a habit of regular reflection and writing, while also enabling teachers to share strategies and ideas. Blogging creates powerful networks that have at their heart both a focus on improving provisions for students in the classroom, and demystifying what happens behind different classroom doors.

It might be, however, that you want to reflect in a more private sphere. Keeping a regular journal or diary to track your experiences in the classroom can be very helpful. As we shall see the next chapter, it can be hugely cathartic and a means by which perspective can be found in the maze of stressful and busy days. The process of reflecting with colleagues in an informal capacity, or with a coach, can also be very helpful if the idea of writing does not appeal to you.

Schedule Time

Regular reflection can be forged by starting a routine. It is best to be realistic and start with something small, such as a ten-minute daily window in which you will pen some thoughts about your day. Doing this for a few weeks will initially be challenging, as you fight the range of other temptations that make up our lives. What it will soon do, however, is become an automatic habit. A few years ago I set myself the goal of writing a reflective diary entry every day for a year; now, it is a habit that is very much embedded in my daily routine.

Identify Questions

It is important to give your reflection some structure and guidance. Identifying core questions and goals that you want to reflect on can help with this aspect. Some example questions are:

1. What aspect of teaching do I want to improve and why?
2. What do I value in the classroom?
3. What makes a positive day in the classroom?
4. What makes a bad day in the classroom?
5. What strategies will I put in place to assist with this?
6. Who will I observe?

In a recent report from Deans for Impact (2016), titled Practice with Purpose, the authors highlight the importance of 'setting goals that are well-defined, specific and measurable'. This means focusing on a particular aspect of teaching rather than looking at 'broad, general improvement'. These goals then build upon each other, progressing from simplistic to more sophisticated targets. We then need to actively seek feedback to build on these goals, using short and focused observations to help.

Reflect on the Positives

There is a misconception that we only need to reflect when things have gone wrong, in order to learn from our mistakes. What will help us to feel more optimistic and self-aware, however, is reflecting on areas in which things have gone positively. Mary Myatt (2016b) makes this clear in *Hopeful Schools*, stating that 'the bottom line is that we all have much more influence than we think we have'. At times, we need to pause and think carefully about the positive steps we are making, to help us to persevere through the more challenging obstacles. This gives us the internal satisfaction of recognising how we are moving forward.

This will also give us the clarity about what we need to simplify in order to do more of the same positive actions. As Peter Drucker (2008) recommends, 'follow effective action with quiet reflection. From the quiet reflection, will come even more effective action'.

Research Informed teaching

There is an abundance of conflicting research about teaching and learning: our earlier evaluation of the merits of learning styles being a prime example. It can often be overwhelming to sift through and find what will help us to improve and grow as practitioners. We cannot expect every decision we make in the classroom to be based on evidence. Yet, engaging with research will have a positive impact in our classroom practice, particularly when it is transferable for our own use. A number of schools are now appointing research leads whose responsibility is to provide practical advice to staff about how research could be effectively implemented in the classroom. As Tom Bennett highlights in his report on Research Leads for the Education Development Trust (2016), their value is to 'create dialogue of challenge where the staff member was forced to revisit their own motivations and evidence base'.

The popularity of both formal and informal conferences, such as 'Research Ed', also highlights how important the role of research is for growing and developing as a classroom practitioner. Hundreds of teachers descend upon such events as a means to share good practice and research informed teaching. It is fuelling this reflective and inquisitive desire to learn more about how to best approach aspects of teaching and learning. Carl Hendrick and Robin Macpherson (2017) highlight in their book on using research in the classroom that 'effective research is a form of liberation which gives teachers a richer vocabulary with which to navigate the complex language of the classroom'.

As this chapter has hopefully demonstrated, our teaching has the exciting potential to slowly improve over time. The fact that the students we teach can continually expect a more refined and developed version of their teachers to arrive each new academic year is inspiring. As Moliere wrote, 'the trees that are slow to grow bear the best fruit'. However, there is no use in ignoring, the most pervasive of teaching emotions that still lurks ominously in the background: namely, stress.

Slow Questions

1. What aspect of your teaching would you value more feedback on?

2. Who have you observed recently that has influenced an aspect of your teaching?

3. Who has observed you teach and what was the impact of their observation?

4. Could you designate more time to reflecting on your impact in the classroom? How would you complete this reflection?

5. What dialogue are you regularly sharing about teaching?

6. Could you act in a coaching capacity for a colleague? Would you benefit from some coaching?

7. Could you engage more in research about teaching?

PART VI: SLOW WELLBEING

CHAPTER 17: UNDERSTANDING AND MANAGING STRESS

Do not anticipate trouble or worry about what may never happen. Keep in the sunlight.
Benjamin Franklin

There is an unhelpful and unattainable view of teaching that is often promoted, which involves complete sacrifice by teachers in the single-minded determination to secure the progress of students. Some schools subliminally advocate this as the way that teachers should function: a relentless marathon of activity that should see us collapse into a heap by a Friday night. 'Teaching is a way of being,' they cry as they leave in the dead of night, wielding sacks of marked books, 'not just a job!'

The excellent English blogger James Theobald (2017) recently took issue with this, exposing the ludicrous nature of some of the maxims that dominate mugs and cards for teachers, all contributing to his conclusion that 'the valorisation of teaching as a form of ritual suicide is subtle and pervasive'. He was particularly scathing about this ubiquitous example: 'A good teacher is like a candle – it consumes itself to light the way for others.' This thoughtless hyperbole undermines the vital examination of work–life balance and stress that is essential for our longevity in the profession. As we shall see in this chapter, we can still maintain a passionate and committed approach to the students we teach; however, this can be achieved by putting our own wellbeing first.

Teacher Burnout

My own experience with managing stress and the pressure of teaching is one of the reasons why I believe such embellishment is an ill-considered and naïve way to view any profession. I was given a range of opportunities during my early years in teaching, becoming an assistant head of a comprehensive school in central London at the age of twenty seven. This was a huge learning curve, but it was a pleasure working and learning alongside a dedicated and committed group of professionals. In reality, however, it was also extremely stressful, as I tried to juggle the various demands of early leadership.

Things came to a tipping point as the first term in my second year in the post came to an end. An Ofsted inspection, a demanding role as head of a large facility, and my own rather obsessive running habit added fuel to the fire. What was more influential was my 'ostrich in the sand' mentality, a single-minded desire to blindly power on. I became extremely run down, picked up a range of illnesses that refused to disappear, but continued to drag myself out of bed every morning to run the three miles into school, arriving at 6am.

Ludicrously, I had prided myself on never taking a day off from teaching: I was young, fit and utterly invincible, and well able to handle working ridiculous hours. My wife was in despair, and urged me (ironically) to slow down and take some time off. I arrogantly rejected this plea, instead working longer and longer hours in a dazed attempt to manage the demands on my shoulders.

Then, I crashed and hit rock bottom.

For weeks I was bed-ridden, completely exhausted and burnt out. I had to take a number of weeks off work (and even more upsettingly, almost a year of no proper running!) and it was a long time before I was anything like my former self. The irony was that this was entirely of my own making; it was my own decisions and actions that meant I drove myself into the ground so spectacularly.

I had a real insight into the reality of how destructive teaching can be, how easy it can 'consume' our lives. Although the school was supportive, I knew that I needed to take a step back from the 'Formula One' route through teaching I had been following. I needed to learn how to manage and cope more efficiently with the stresses and strains of what, I hope, will be a long career in education.

The Reality of Stress

As a profession, stress is something that we frequently talk about, but in reality most have little understanding of how it functions, and a lack of strategies to deal positively with its consequences. There is also, dare I say it, a degree of hyperbole surrounding stress. Legions of self-help books promise to 'Overcome stress now' or 'Remove stress from your life' and we often huddle in staffrooms vocalising about how overwhelmingly stressed we are. Clearly, this is unhelpful; stress will always be a part of life and to try to magically dissipate it, or to constantly bemoan its presence, will only make us feel more anxious. Stress is a perfectly normal human emotion; in fact, it is an essential human emotion.

Walter Cannon, a physiologist, was the first to identify the concept of the 'fight or flight response' (1915) in relation to the impact of stress. It is primarily a physical response, in which the body switches itself to 'fight or flight' mode when faced with a situation, in turn reducing a range of hormones and chemicals such as adrenaline and cortisol in the body. Clearly, there are benefits to this happening; benefits which our cavemen ancestors exploited, allowing them to escape from dangerous situations. Our body is very sensitive to these hormones, which is why we feel our heart race and our body tighten when faced with teaching a class that give us sleepless nights.

In order to manage these feelings, however, we should avoid fixating on them or viewing stress as purely negative or destructive. Kelly McGonigal (2015) notes that 'Stress happens when something you care about is at stake. It's not a sign to run away – it's a sign to step forward'. Stress is a signal that we are emotionally engaged and invested in what we are doing and want to do it to the best of our ability. If we channel such short-term stress appropriately it can, in fact, aid the energy and passion with which we approach our work. Without feelings of stress we would face an almost robotic path through life; a sure passport to a monotonous and unfulfilling existence.

The problem is when we become stressed too often, when we are continuously in this state of 'flight'. Our bodies, as I discovered, are not able to deal with sustained and chronic long-term stress. We need to be able to recognise the distinctions between helpful and unavoidable stress, and long-term stress which leaves us overwhelmed, unable to sleep and emotionally volatile. To do this we need to be able to monitor our emotions.

Building Self-Awareness

During the transition from a life of frantic pace in London to a full-time teaching role in the more restrained North-East, I was determined to make more time for reflection and thought. But this is by no means easy, with the daily range of interactions and dizzying expectations of life in the school environment, detaching one's self to observe emotion is challenging.

Developing greater self-awareness by recognising our responses in situations and adopting our actions appropriately can help us to build emotional resilience. When we find ourselves becoming stressed, we should instead begin to employ some of the strategies that can calm us and provide us with perspective, an approach which we will explore over the next few chapters.

If those feelings of continuous stress persevere, then we need to take proactive steps to ask for support: our colleagues, friends, family or external agencies may all be able to help. Schools have a number of avenues to facilitate this support, and while it may be a difficult step, the lightness we feel after conversations can fuel our spirits. We begin to gain a vital filter from our clouded judgement, helping us to find solutions and alternatives to the difficulties we are experiencing. Being able to work with these feelings, rather than fighting against them, will also help us to feel more confident and in charge of our work in schools.

Teacher Confidence

One of the reasons stress can become pervasive and overwhelming is when there is a lack of confidence in our own efficiency in the work place. It is why the NQT year, or the first year we are in a new role with responsibility, can be so demanding. The irony is that the perceived evil twins of doubt and insecurity can in fact nourish and improve us as teachers. In reality most of us fluctuate wildly when it comes to confidence, as Alex Quigley (2016) notes in this encouraging and normalising extract from *The Confident Teacher*:

> One of the lessons that emerge from my professional experience with colleagues is that many of the best teachers are bursting with brilliance, but they can easily struggle with a seemingly shallow well of self-confidence. Like Bertrand Russell stated, they are full of doubts, about themselves and their ability to teach well.

Doubt is clearly useful in fuelling our desire to improve, but we cannot let it become corrosive. Getting regular feedback about our performance is vital to help reassure us about our work. If feedback is not provided, then we need to be proactive and seek out those conversations to gain clarity about what is required. Doubts need to be balanced with appropriate perspective; we often need to remind ourselves about the good we do in our professional capacity. Earlier points about taking the time to celebrate positives, as well as giving ourselves space to work on the areas we want to develop on, will help in this respect.

Teacher Perfectionism

It is also important to recognise that teaching is a perfectionist's greatest enemy: there will always be more to do, an endless task list that we will never conquer. Often, managerial decisions (or idealised visions of a teacher's capacity to work twenty-four hours a day) can feed this endless cycle. Like most professions, realising that we cannot possibly win in the never-ending battle to get to the end of our to-do list is one important aspect of being able to cope and beginning to thrive.

Instead of listening to the pernickety call of the perfectionist, we need to ruthlessly prioritise and learn how to maintain a healthy perspective. It is important to develop a sense of discipline, which is why embracing what Chris Eyre (2016) defines as the 'fifty is plenty' solution for classroom teachers may be a sensible idea.

We hear frequent horror stories of teachers working sixty or seventy-hour weeks. Clearly this is unsustainable and one of the reasons why many good teachers leave, exhausted by the profession. Eyre (2016) argues that in imposing a limit of fifty hours a week, we sharpen our time management and make sure that we do not spend too long on tasks. We also start to filter our thinking about whether the time we are spending at work will impact positively on our students. By imposing such limitations we also avoid the temptation to behave like teaching is an endless profession; there needs to be a cut-off point at some stage. It is younger and less experienced members of staff that need more explicit guidance on how to manage this process or prioritising, particularly if we want to build a more attractive and sustainable vision of teaching.

Wheel of Balance

Another reason why stress can become overwhelming is when we fall into the trap of 'treadmill teaching': always moving and always working. Without the necessary balance in our lives, we begin to adopt a particularly blinkered perspective in which the demands of teaching start to dominate our personal lives. As George Bernard Shaw (2013) said 'one of the symptoms of approaching nervous breakdown is the belief that one's work is terribly important'.

In the midst of a particularly frantic academic term, it is vital to pause and assess our 'wheel of balance'. We can do this by drawing a pie chart on a sheet of blank paper and filling in how much of our time is invested in each area of our lives: for example, work, family, friends, hobbies etc. This can be visually shocking as we see just how much of our time is ensnared by work. It is important that we step outside of the temptation to define ourselves as being just 'a teacher'. The more variety and happiness we have in our lives, the more we can cope with the demands of stress, and develop the joyous optimism that will sustain us through more challenging periods.

If we allow it to, teaching can begin to dominate every moment of our waking (and sleeping!) life. Embracing a hobby or something outside of the world of teaching has significant benefits. There is a completely unfounded feeling of guilt that sometimes hovers over teachers if they step off the teaching treadmill during term time.

I have known colleagues who partake in some spectacular hobbies, from as far-reaching as bird watching to karate. The teachers who are most effective in the classroom are the ones who radiate with the qualities of lifelong learning and are genuinely interesting and energising. Finding an activity that takes us outside of our internal fretting can help us to return with a calm, focused mind and a renewed sense of drive. Running (somewhat detracting from this book's title!) has always been my fix; there is nothing like it to cleanse the mind and body at the end of a long day. Exercise in its many different forms can generate those positive endorphins that will make us feel better equipped to manage the stress and strain of life.

Perspective

We are in control of how our mind is functioning, no matter how busy the world appears around us. This is the principle thesis of *The Things You Can See Only When You Slow Down* (2017) by Haemin Sunim, in which the author argues that by slowing down our mindset, we profoundly influence our view of the world around us. As Sunim notes:

> The world is experienced according to the state of one's mind. When your mind is joyful and compassionate, the world is, too. When your mind is filled with negative thoughts, the world appears negative, too. When you feel overwhelmed and busy, remember that you are not powerless. When your mind rests, the world also rests.

There might be a temptation to speed up in response to the diverse demands we face, but to do so will only lead to ineffective outcomes and exhaustion, burnout or, at the very least, dissatisfaction. Indeed, deliberately slowing down will enable a more joyful, easeful and calm perspective.

The truth is that those who are most respected in any professional environment have an ethereal quality; they radiate calm purposefulness and appear utterly unable to be jolted by the events of the day. Students are aware when they are in the hands of a teacher like this and, in turn, they feel confident and assured by their presence.

One way to help develop this sense of peace and ease with the pressures we face in education is to broaden our perspectives. Teaching can, if we are honest, be a rather insular profession at times. There is also, perhaps inevitably, a degree of negativity which we can find ourselves sucked into the vortex of.

Taking the time to step outside of this and recognise the plethora of demands others' face and deal with on a daily basis can be enable us to gather perspective. One of the best things I have read which illuminates this theory was an interview with former president Barack Obama interview on the value of reading at the close of his presidency in *The New York Times*:

"At a time when events move so quickly and so much information is transmitted" He said, reading gave him the ability to occasionally "slow down and get perspective" and "the ability to get in somebody else's shoes". "Whether they have made me a better president I can't say. But what I can say is they have allowed me to sort of maintain my balance during the course of eight years, because this is a place that comes at you hard and fast and doesn't let up (Kakutani, 2017).

He goes on to outline how reading about others' experiences, 'counters the tendency to think that whatever is going on right now is uniquely disastrous or amazing or difficult'. While we don't quite have the same level of stress that Mr Obama was under in the throes of his presidency, reading can nonetheless be a hugely positive in forging a path to manage our own stress.

Communication and Collaboration

One of the aspects that can increase feelings of stress is the isolated nature of teaching. We are the captains of a range of ships that can often appear to be ours and only ours. What can help us to manage these feelings of stress and isolation are those who may be experiencing exactly the same things as us: our colleagues.

The time we spend with the colleagues around us can be one of the things that brings us joy in the workplace. It can be lonely work when our primary mode of communication is with adolescents. Stepping outside of this and taking the time to have an 'adult' chat can rejuvenate a tired spirit. Every staffroom also has its own sage or dispassionate oracle, someone who can provide guidance on how to maintain a sense of perspective and who can alleviate the sense of panic and stress that can ripple through schools like wildfire.

Teaching is a stressful job; there is no escaping that reality. It requires us to give significant energy and work hard for bursts at a time, all while juggling a number of demands. Yet, our self-awareness and capacity to manage our emotions makes a significant difference on how we respond to these daily challenges. Our ability to be open, set limitations and maintain perspective can stop stress overtaking us. The next chapter will look more specifically at the tricks of the teaching trade, the wellbeing essentials that will also align with our new ethereal, calm attitude.

Slow Questions

1. Are you at risk of burnout?

2. What is your relationship like with stress?

3. What strategies are you using to manage feelings of stress?

4. Are you using the support network of colleagues in school?

5. Are you conscious of the perfectionism trap?

6. Could you build in more optimism into both your internal and external presence in school?

CHAPTER 18: ARMING OURSELVES AGAINST ANXIETY

It always seems impossible until it is done.
Nelson Mandela

Anxiety can strike teachers frequently. Often, we fixate on how challenging our class will be in the next lesson; or, we begin to feel overwhelmed as we see the huge amount of marking we need to get through; or, we fret about those intimidating performance management targets. In a recent NASUWT survey (2016) of 5,000 teachers, over three quarters (79%) of respondents reported experiencing work-related anxiousness. That revelation will, as Daniel Goleman *et al* (2003) suggest, have an adverse impact on how well we work. As the authors note, 'negative emotions – especially chronic anger, anxiety or a sense of futility – powerfully disrupt work, hijacking attention from the task at hand'.

There are certain anxiety trigger points throughout the school year: the start of the term, the exam season, laborious report writing and endless data analysis. Much of what this book has covered will hopefully be helpful to you in coping with feelings of anxiety: embracing the minimalistic and organised environment; streamlining teaching; employing a consistent and calm approach to managing behaviour; using school support networks; being strategic about what we mark; working on understanding our relationship with stress. Combined with these there are, however, some practical ways in which we can dissipate the anxiety that leaves us tense at the end of the working day.

Organisation and Chunking

A typical consequence of stress and anxiety is that we begin to see things through tunnel vision, losing the ability to gain perspective or plan in advance. This negatively impacts both our interactions with students and our sense of clarity about the best approaches for teaching. One way to alleviate such feelings, as explored in Chapter 3, is to plan carefully and strategically for the future.

Having real clarity about the potential pressure points in a school year can help us immeasurably in our ability to plan, thus avoiding feelings of panic. Breaking our school year into chunks which we can plan for in advance will set us up for a focused academic year. A utilised staff planner can be a delightful stress alleviator to help with this.

Using a checklist or a plan for the day or week will mean we can prioritise our tasks when other things inevitably arise. Harry Fletcher-Wood (2016) outlines the various merits of checklists in *Ticked off: Checklists for Teachers, Students, School Leaders*, noting that a checklist will give us a real sense of transparency and will help us to work systematically through the various things we need to complete to feel more in control. This will also help us to make the most of the valuable free periods we have in school. These periods can often disappear in a haze; therefore, effective planning will help us to make the most of this breathing space, and not leave us frustrated at what we perceive as lost time.

The Start of the Academic Year

September starts can present many situations that fuel anxiety: new groups, new timetables and new names to learn. It is also one of the most physically exhausting times, as we try to sustain high levels of energy and enthusiasm in the mission to inspire new groups of students. This anxiety is heightened due to the contrast with the weeks of unruffled serenity we've had during the holidays. The brain instantly goes into overdrive with the increased level of activity as we return to work. Some tips to manage this effectively are:

1. **Plan in advance:** There is real clarity in using the last week of the break to think through the first two weeks of the school year, and to have clear plans for the term ahead. While it may eat into the end of our summer holidays, it means we can focus on the other demands of the new school year and, ultimately, will save us time. Prioritising the development of a comprehensive understanding of new groups as quickly as possible will also help. What are their starting points and who will you need to be pushing from the start of the year?

2. **It is a marathon not a sprint:** At the beginning of the year it is important to be patient with yourself and recognise that you will not be able to morph immediately back into your teacher persona. The school year is a long one; there is plenty of time to fit back into that mode of operation that will feel utterly seamless again within weeks. Earlier points about the dangers of perfectionism are particularly important here. Remember: it is vital to be patient and understanding with yourself.

3. **Initial lessons with a group do not define the year:** Even if the first lesson with a new class is an utter disaster, there will be plenty of time to develop the relationships you want with them. Sometimes, there are classes who decide

to test us straight away. Applying a consistent and calm stoical behavioural management approach will soon have them on side and on task. Investing in securing this at the start of the year requires real energy, but will pay off.

4. **Get parents on side:** I was encouraged at the beginning of my career to engage with parents as quickly as possible at the start of the academic year. It means you can have some lovely upbeat introductory phone conversations to open the new term. Students see that you mean business and parents will have a positive impression of your commitment to their child. If things don't continue so positively, you have already built up a bank of good will.

Parents' Evenings

Meetings with parents can be stressful situations, particularly when we may need to be less positive than parents might ideally wish for. There is the inevitable close perusal of us; we are, after all, in charge of their child's academic future in our subject. Making a positive impression and keeping calm can be achieved by the following methods:

1. **Smile:** Interpersonal skills come into force here. Showing parents we enjoy teaching their child and are positive in their presence will help us to gain their trust and support. Smiling can be one of our best weapons against stress and anxiety, releasing positive endorphins because your brain immediately connects it with happiness. Trying this first thing in the morning can set us up for a day of tranquillity.

2. **Have evidence:** Building up evidence to support any points about work or behaviour is very useful. This can take many different forms: workbooks, school logs of behaviour, or feedback from other teachers. If, for example, a student is demonstrating laziness, having a comparative student example at hand will help to illustrate how they should be exerting more effort.

3. **Script it:** As with any aspect of teaching, the more we script our key points for difficult parental meetings, the more we can provide confident clarity. Even having some key bullet points for the more difficult conversations will make us feel calmer.

The Exam Season

One of the most stressful times of the school year is the weeks leading up to final exams. Schools often become full of anxiety, as students prepare themselves for what is among the first stressful landmarks in their lives. Making sure we can appropriately manage, or indeed mask, our own well-intentioned feelings of anxiety about how our students will perform at this point is crucial. Some ways to achieve this are:

1. The 'graceful swan effect': In *The Confident Teacher* (2016), Alex Quigley explores what he deems as 'the graceful swan effect':

> That is to say, you are harried and busy, struggling with feelings of 'imposter syndrome', but you act as graceful as a swan. It doesn't deny that feelings of doubt are real. It doesn't eliminate our stresses. Crucially, however, it is a reminder that masking our fears are necessary and that people want to have confidence in their colleagues and leaders.

It is the perfect analogy for the exam period. The more we can present an attitude of calm and collective confidence, the more our students will mirror these feelings. We also start to believe in the authenticity of what may indeed be an act, helping us to feel more relaxed.

2. Direction: There is nothing worse for students, or indeed teachers, than last-minute, panicked lessons that radiate this sense of examination fear. All this does is increase the stress and pressure that both we and our students feel. Teaching huge amounts of additional intervention to tired students at the end of the day will only leave them, and us, feeling more frazzled. We both need to sustain the energy for the time we have in lessons. Again, the more carefully we have planned each lesson, and the better organised and purposeful each homework task has been throughout the year, the more confident our students will feel that they are prepared effectively. At this time of year, investing energy into preparing lessons to check understanding and get students to actively demonstrate their knowledge will be more useful that an additional forty-five minutes a week intervention.

3. Motivate: During the exams, rather than give into the temptation to berate students about their lack of work or perceived failures, we need to find moments to celebrate the positives and the effort they are putting in. Like all of us, our students are more receptive to optimism and positivity, as it will make them realise that they can achieve whatever they are setting their minds to. It is more likely to motivate those who are not working as hard as they could be. If every teacher adopts this approach in exam session, then students will be calm and buoyed going into their exams.

Embrace the Collaboration

There is often far too much isolation in the modern school environment. I know that I myself would benefit from embracing more of a John Donne philosophy to life in teaching – 'no man is an island/entire of itself/every man is a piece of the continent/a part of the main'. Schools can often replicate and repeat work that, if we took more time to share and communicate, could significantly reduce workload. Some useful ways in which collaboration can help with the demands and leave anxiety behind are:

1. **Collaborative knowledge organisers:** As we saw in Chapter 3, knowledge organisers that outline the skills required in a unit give us a sense of clarity about the direction of half a term or a full academic year. The more we combine our understanding of topics, the easier the planning for the term becomes and the less uncertainty we feel. It is all about sharing the expertise and experience that will make up a department. While we need to have ownership over the content of our own individual lessons, embracing the collaborative approach for long-term planning is a much more sensible. Pulling together the collective resources from a department to help teaching improve overall will facilitate a sense of common purpose.

2. **Collaborative assessment and marking:** The process of grading and marking assessments is – particularly with a change of specification – rather intimidating and stressful. The more this is done in departmental teams, the more secure we can be in our judgements and the less we feel the hazy indecision that can fuel anxiety. This clarity and confidence will then feed into our lessons and our interactions with students.

3. **Collaborative behaviour management:** The best departments work relentlessly to support each other in the drive to ensure that students sustain excellent behaviour. This removes the individual battle focus and makes behaviour a more collective responsibility. Departmental detentions are very empowering in this regard.

4. **Team spirit:** The best departments have an inspiring team collective; they pull together both emotionally and practically in order to do the best for students. They recognise and exploit the different strengths that each individual can bring to the team, using this to inform CPD and the support network that will run through a department.

Performance Management Targets

Did we really come into teaching in order to achieve targets on a spreadsheet? Is the time we spend agonising over whether our students will hit three or four levels of progress time well spent? Having an understanding of varying targets and where students should be by the end of the year is, of course, important. It is, however, all about perspective. Those spreadsheet targets should remain firmly in the background of our thinking, and instead our focus should be to get on with the business of teaching and learning.

What is more essential is that we consider carefully how we can teach these individual students and lead them to a successful end point. By organising and planning carefully for their success, and teaching with passion, thought and enthusiasm, we are on the path for doing the very best for these students. We have already explored the profound complexities of young people, and the target grade must never replace the understanding we are trying to build of a student and their strengths and weaknesses.

Streamlining data also needs to be a focus for us as individual classroom teachers. As a numerically challenged English teacher, data collections always inspire fear of the unknown from me. Making sure we receive guidance on what exactly our data means for our students is important. Using it sensibly in our classroom to inform planning will help to make it meaningful. Then is up to those in positions of responsibility to make sure that we are not overburdened with endless data collections that detract from more meaningful ways to use our time.

Tackling Inspections

One of the most stressful aspects of teaching is the ominous threat of Ofsted that lurks over schools. Whatever teachers think of their workplace, there has to be accountability at all levels of education, and Ofsted is the mechanism that ensures this. Endless complaining is wasted energy; all we can do is channel this into making sure we prepare effectively and efficiently.

1. **Avoid the obsession:** It would be foolish to ignore Ofsted, but there are schools that are fixated with it, and seem to orchestrate everything in order to fulfil the latest Ofsted agenda. Their walls are draped in Ofsted hyperbole, which appears to define it more than the students within their walls. This isn't fair to staff or students; treating education like a performance for an external agency only increases the sense of fear about its presence. We need to be actively aware of Ofsted, not use it to justify every new policy or direction.

2. **Read the reports:** To help us understand what Ofsted will be looking for if they enter our classroom, a useful strategy is to digest and reflect on Ofsted guidance and reports collaboratively in our departments. It is about being proactive, ensuring that as teachers and departments you are 'Ofsted-proof' in advance, rather than frantically running around to prepare in the hours after receiving that dreaded call. It could be as simple as knowing exactly what you

have to provide if an inspector enters your lesson: a continuously changing conundrum.

3. **Surviving the inspection:** There is a new level of anxiety that overcomes a school during an Ofsted inspection, particularly if the culture of the school is driven by Ofsted fear. It is important to remember that the great majority of students will be on your side and will want to see the school, and you, do well. Alongside this, it is vital to have confidence and faith in what you do on a daily basis and avoid all temptation to change the dynamic and structure of how you teach. Remember that Ofsted have announced that they don't want to see a particular style of teaching. Trying to do something out of your normal routines will only make both you, and your students, feel more anxious.

Dealing with Setbacks

Unfortunately, the school year will not seamlessly reveal success after success. There will be challenges and difficulties experienced throughout the year. Learning to embrace these challenges and use them positively will help us to avoid becoming overwhelmed. Returning to our stoical philosophy from earlier can help us to maintain a sense of perspective; we can and will bounce back from any disappointments. Marcus Aurelius' (2004) wisdom will always be reassuring: 'Be like the rocky headland on which the waves constantly break. It stands firm, and round it the seething waters are laid to rest'.

There are very few positives that self-castigating ourselves can serve. Remembering that mistakes and setbacks are an essential part of the process of learning, and allowing ourselves time to pause and gain perspective will help us to manage any disappointments. Importantly, it will also help us to bounce back from mistakes and make improvements.

People Pressure

Sometimes it is not the students that make life hard in school; occasionally, it can be our interactions with colleagues. There are those in the educational world who expect us to work relentlessly, and seem to be infuriatingly unable to be reflective about what is best for staff or students. In the face of this, learning to say 'no' is a vital skill in any workplace. Sometimes we are respected more because of our capacity to draw the line and state why we will not be able to complete something.

It is important that we are assertive in our school environment, speaking up when we feel that something is not functioning effectively and having those difficult conversations, when needed. This is not about being hostile or demonstrating arrogance; it is about being true to our own professional integrity. If we are not open about them, frustrations are much more likely to build up and impact how we feel about our work.

Stress becomes more pervasive, much louder and much fiercer when we are lacking in the magical ingredient of sleep. We know how replenished and energised we feel in the morning when we are rested. Without it we begin to morph into a particularly manic version of Shakespeare's Macbeth, as Lady Macbeth turns to him and cries 'you lack the season of all natures, sleep'. To avoid this (or indeed descending into the later sleepwalking Lady Macbeth) we should look closely at how to improve our relationship with the pillow...

Slow Questions

1. Do you have a clear grasp of the potential anxiety trigger points in the year?

2. Have you got an action plan for the first two weeks of the new academic year?

3. Are you using the checklist approach to planning for your day and week?

4. Are you planning for parental meetings to help feel calm and be prepared?

5. Is collaboration high up on your agenda?

6. How can you ensure calm clarity during the exam season?

7. Are you confidently informed and ready for an Ofsted inspection?

CHAPTER 19: TACKING TEACHER INSOMNIA: SLEEP EASY

The whole world is time-sick. We all belong to the same cult of speed.
Carl Honore

In our relentlessly fast modern culture, there is one aspect of life that is tragically ignored. It refuses to conform to speed and certainly does not embrace the twenty-four-hour, 'always on' lifestyle. It is perceived to be an inconvenience by some, a waste of precious and valuable time.

It is the much overlooked and much undervalued quality of sleep.

To function on very little sleep is becoming more of a feature in modern Britain; indeed, for some, it becomes a kind of badge of honour, which adds to the glorification of busy, to loudly proclaim their ability to 'thrive' on five hours sleep. In the *Great British Sleep Survey (2012)*, a study spanning two years and over 20,000 people, a third of respondents reported that they slept for less than six hours a night. The average recommended sleeping time for adults is between seven and eight hours in order to remain fully functional; therefore, it is clear that many British citizens are coming up consistently short.

Teacher Sleep

As teachers we are arguably rather near the top of the sleep spurning pile. With the plethora of time-guzzling demands on our shoulders, we go evening by evening rejecting the call of the pillow. The disjointed nature of our work also fuels sleeping issues. We survive in highly focused short bursts of term time, in which the amount we need to get through is intensive. We fluctuate from being intensely 'on' during term, to replenishing our sleep patterns during our much-needed breaks. The consequence of this is highly disrupted sleeping patterns, and a confused body clock. These sporadic sleeping patterns can have a real impact on our efficiency, not only in the workplace but also as a functioning adult.

I share what is without doubt a widespread teacher issue: I have a rather troublesome relationship with sleep. My slumber efficiency was never ideal, but came to an ugly head in my late twenties with an unwelcome two years of broken and miserable sleep. I know what a profoundly depressing and difficult thing it is to survive on very little sleep; how it can lead to a vicious cycle of anxiety and poor functioning.

Sleep issues manifest in a variety of ways. Mine was the dreaded early morning awakening, with 5am for a long time officially defined as a lie-in. In the attempt to improve this rather miserable cycle, I have developed a rather obsessional archive of sleep-related knowledge. (I make particularly spectacular dinner party company.) I haven't quite reached, however, the dizzying heights of Charles Dickens, whose obsession with getting a good sleep led to him sleeping in the exact centre of a mattress and ensuring the bed was facing north. As you can imagine, this was woefully unsuccessful and he ended up spending the wee hours wandering around London; although on a positive note, that did inspire some rather magnificent writing.

Teenage Sleeping

If you are one of those fortunate individuals who is blessed with the ability to sleep like a baby at even the most stressful of times, the reality is that a great deal of the students we teach are completely rejecting the need for sleep. By arming ourselves with sleep hygiene knowledge, we can become a Gandalf-style oracle of sleep wisdom. We can help to guide them on why it is vital to prioritise getting enough sleep and provide them with practical tips.

Sleep Issues

Problems with sleeping can feel like a hugely isolating experience, an issue that intensifies the more we fixate on it. There is comfort and a normalising aspect to knowing that lots of people struggle with this aspect of life. Here are the typical sleep problems as stated by Dr Nerina Ramlakhan (2016). Take a deep breath:

- Difficulty getting to sleep or sleep initiation problems.

- Difficulty staying asleep or sleep maintenance issues.

- Sleeping but feeling as if you're not sleeping (mentally busy, 'tired but wired' sleep) – this is called paradoxical insomnia.

- Oversleeping or hypersomnia and still feeling exhausted.

- Restlessness and restless let syndrome (RLS).

- Parasomnia such as sleepwalking, sleep talking, nightmares, night terrors or teeth grinding (bruxism).

- Delayed sleep phase syndrome, where you can't get to sleep until late – technology often plays a bit part here.

- Circadian rhythm sleep disorder – typically due to shift working.

The reality is that we bring the experience of our days to bed with us. Sleeping is certainly not something that happens in isolation – divorced from our behaviour for the time we are awake. Inevitably, a more holistic process of slowing down will have a significant impact on our ability to 'switch off' and fall gracefully into the arms of a pillow at the end of our long teaching days. Even if we follow all the sleep-easy tips to come, if we fly through our days in a blur of cortisone and stress, our minds will not drift into sleep.

The Value of Sleep

Richard Wiseman (2015) notes that 'one way of examining the role that sleep plays in your life would involve preventing you ever from sleeping, and then seeing what happens to your brain and body'. Wiseman discusses his involvement with a television show *Shattered* (recorded in 2004) in which the contestant who stayed awake for the longest won £100,000. Inevitably, the widespread psychological and physical damage in the show did not lead to a repeat series. Wiseman concluded that 'the suffering endured by those who have attempted to remain continuously awake for several days vividly demonstrated humanities deep-seated need for sleep'.

Initially, it is simple: sleep is how we protect our brains, replenish and recover from the demands of the day (of which, in teaching, there are many!) Sleeping is also the means by which our learning and memory consolidates. During sleep the brain goes through synaptic rejuvenation, which is the process by which we consolidate information we have gathered throughout the day.

The Consequences of Inadequate Sleep

The clock ticks dangerously towards midnight, but we are surrounded by a collection of marking and a to-do list that brings tears to the eyes. Another long night ahead, sleep can wait. Caffeine will do the job instead.

By going through this rather predictable evening routine and frequently starving ourselves of sleep, we do a number of detrimental things to our bodies and minds. Interestingly, they are all correlated with what makes us effective practitioners in the classroom: memory, energy and emotional control.

1. **Emotional regulation:** All the calming qualities we need as teachers are severely impacted when we have failed to sleep well. We become much more fractured and irritable, lashing out in ways that we would previously be able to manage and control. Sleep deprivation has a real impact on negative and positive stimulus, resulting in greater activity in the limbic area of the brain, the area where much of the emotional regulation and processing occurs. Our capacity to be stoical and maintain a sense of perspective is utterly shattered without sleep.

2. **Forgetfulness:** We all know that dazed, confused feeling that dominates us if we have had a dreadful night sleep. Without sleep we lose our capacity to organise as efficiently. What is normally an easy problem becomes an insurmountable obstacle, as we struggle to think strategically.

3. **Lack of energy and enthusiasm:** It is difficult enough to sustain our energy levels for a six-period day when we are performing at our best. When we have failed to sleep, it becomes a Herculean task; inevitably one that we cannot sustain. This results in our lessons taking a slump in terms of the energy levels. It doesn't take a genius to work out that when we are tired, we are short tempered, fractured and more inclined to negativity.

Sleep Easy Solutions

Structure

Consistency is a real winner when it comes to sleep. While the temptation is to use weekends to embrace a full, sloth-like forty-eight hours of sleep, it will merely serve to throw our fragile body clocks completely off kilter. The best sleep hygiene includes regular sleep and wake schedules, even on weekends. Our bodies crave consistency, and setting a sleeping structure and sticking to it, as far as possible, will help us to get into a real pattern of effective sleeping.

Exercise

As we have seen in Chapter 17, the benefits of exercise would suggest it has the potential to become a teacher's best friend. It has a hugely positive impact in improving both sleep quality and duration. It doesn't have to involve spending hours slogging in a gym either; anything that raises the heart rate for thirty minutes or so will be useful in helping us to drift off into sleep oblivion.

What is particularly effective is exercising early in morning; the natural sunlight is useful, setting up our body clocks for a day of activity and a night of sleep. A brisk walk first thing in the morning is an excellent way to set us up for the day ahead. Avoiding exercise after 9pm is also helpful; it will leave us too full of adrenaline to calm our minds before sleep. Aches and pains can also be troublesome in impacting our sleep, and regular exercise can have the added benefit of improving flexibility and reducing soreness. Gentle exercise such as yoga or pilates can be hugely beneficial in this regard.

Curb the Electronic Devices

Our phones, tablets, laptops and televisions are ubiquitous and addictive villains in the sleep-easy mission. Unbeknown to us, they omit a sneaky blue light that can have a real impact on our ability to fall asleep. Light in general can stop us feeling tired, going against our bodies attempts to switch itself off.

The blue light from our mobiles and computers actually suppresses the production of melatonin, the hormone that influences our sleep cycles (our circadian rhythm). They are also ruthlessly addictive: there is a flash of adrenaline every time we receive a message or a status update. This build-up of adrenaline leaves us wired and unable to calm ourselves down appropriately to get to sleep, particularly for the more sensitive sleep minds.

The best approach to allow our brains to slow down is to completely curb the electronic devices at least one hour before we go to bed. That means all aspects: including a cheeky check of social media. Being disciplined and avoiding hours on social media throughout the day will also stabilise moods and prevent us from becoming too wired.

Instead of using electronic devices to help leave behind the stress and strains of the day, embracing the comfort of a warm bath can help us drift into a peaceful sleep. The fact that it raises our body temperature, then rapidly cools it down immediately afterwards, has a relaxing impact.

Bedroom Conditions

The bedroom ideally needs to feel like an oasis of sleep. It needs a serious approach: the minimalist cleanse is, again, useful to apply to the bedroom in order to make sure it is a calming and soothing space. Trying to sneak those student books in with us, and marking furiously until the moment we put out the light, will lead only to a broken sleep. On a more extreme level, the mobile and laptops could be banished from the bedroom completely and never permitted entry. What may also sound like very simplistic advice is, in fact, important: only go to bed when you feel tired. Forcing yourself to go to sleep earlier will result in either an early morning rise, or growing frustration as you toss and turn.

Cut Down the Caffeine

Ramlakhan (2016) suggests that research implies we can cope with 400 milligrams of caffeine a day. Take another deep breath and cast your eyes on the amount of caffeine in each of the following:

Cup of instant coffee: 80–100mg

Cup of homemade filter coffee: 150–200mg

Cup of commercial coffee (Costa or Starbucks): 350mg

Cup of tea: 40–80mg

Green tea: 20–30mg

Can of Coke: 30–50mg

Can of energy drink: 80mg.

(Ramlakhan, 2016)

Now, to confound the shock, the half-life (the time it takes to half the concentration in your blood of caffeine) is five hours. That means if you decide to have an early evening coffee at 6pm, half of the caffeine is still floating around your system at 11pm, just when you might be heading off to sleep. The consequence of this is a disrupted sleep cycle.

As teachers, we rank fairly high up on the caffeine-abuse hitlist, with coffee ingested to power us through the day in our quickly snatched breaks. The issue with this is we are giving ourselves energy that is manufactured and will inevitably lead to a caffeine slump; one of the reasons why our loved ones despair at our lack of energy or conversation at the end of the day. Having tried and failed miserably to cut out caffeine completely for some time now, instead here are some practical and manageable tips that I have managed to implement and go some way in lessening the addiction.

1. **Try to slowly cut your caffeine intact:** Trying to go cold turkey abruptly will inevitably prove to be too challenging, with withdrawn headaches and the irritability not particularly pleasant. The mere sniff of coffee beans will see us fly into a withdrawal rage. Instead, make small and manageable steps to cut it down and try to progressively reduce your intake over a number of weeks and months.

2. **Look for coffee alternatives:** Moving to the purifying value of water instead of a coffee will help to make us feel less stressed and wired (and also have a monetary saving impact!) Having decaffeinated tea or coffee, or a delightful herbal alternative, will also relax us instead. Although it may not be particularly hedonistic, a cup of peppermint tea can set us off for a pleasant slumber.

3. **Avoid caffeine after 3pm:** This will result in your system being completely purified by the time you go to bed. The same is true with food; it is sensible to avoid spiking your blood sugar levels before you go to bed by eating, as this will leave your digestive system working hard. Alcohol has a similar impact: although it may initially make you drowsy, it has the impact of disrupting sleep patterns throughout the night.

Deal with Worries

In the Great British Sleep Survey (2012), 82% of respondents said the main thing that kept them awake at night was endless ruminating about 'what happened today and what have I got on tomorrow'. Going to bed with our minds' full of our many and widespread woes, be it to do with teaching or not, will only fuel another fractured night's sleep. Being proactive and recognising that we are tired, but ultimately wired, is the first positive step.

An excellent strategy is to write a list an hour or so before going to bed, highlighting the things that we need to do the next day. Once we see this in written form, it provides perspective and helps us to organise and crystallise our thinking for the next day. We then have time to leave this behind as we prepare for sleep; much better than swimming in the elevated feelings of panic that lying awake at night can generate. If writing doesn't help, the simple process of vocalising our concerns and talking them through with someone will help us to find perspective. Anything that removes the internal fretting will help.

Recognising how much and how well we are sleeping is vital in impacting our efficiency and effectiveness. What will be most helpful for the students we teach is presenting the best version of ourselves in the classroom. Doing this requires us to prioritise our rest. Staying up till 2am marking books will only result in exhaustion and irritability; we need to be kind and compassionate to ourselves.

There is one other excellent way in which we can begin to fend off our stress, anxiety and sleep demons; it is time to embrace some Zen-inspired meditation serenity.

Slow Questions

1. What is your relationship with sleep like? Are you getting enough?

2. Do you have a sleeping routine that you are sticking to?

3. Could you reduce your caffeine intake?

4. Is your bedroom a haven for sleep?

5. Do you need to curb your use of electronic devices?

6. Could you make time for more exercise to improve your wellbeing and sleep?

7. Are you addressing worries proactively before going to sleep?

CHAPTER 20: EMBRACING MINDFULNESS: THE MEDITATING AND MINDFUL TEACHER

Meditation is not evasion; it is a serene encounter with reality.
Thich Nhat Hanh

As we have seen throughout this slow journey through education, the internal mind wars of a teacher can be rather overwhelming. There are, as with any profession, a range of demands clambering for our attention. Yet, not many jobs have the loud and immediate calls of what can often amount to over a hundred young people. Given what appears to be an insurmountable workload, we are reluctant to invest any time that is purely for ourselves. To take any free time to do so would be yet another example of leaving behind our families or friends.

The Ten-Minute Solution

No matter how frantically busy we may perceive ourselves to be, we can always find ten minutes that can be designated to ourselves. Spending this time in quiet contemplation can have a hugely positive result, not only our wellbeing, but also on our capacity to gain perspective. It will also help us to pause momentarily and escape from the relentless pace of life and teaching, a vital endeavour for our long-term health.

A few years ago, the concept of mindfulness and meditation was one I would youthfully scoff at: there was no way you would find me wasting my time 'sitting around'. Indeed, there will be many who might approach this chapter with the same frame of mind, the perfectly understandable cynicism and doubt that we employ for the things outside of our everyday experience. Yet, the evidence on the emotional impact of embracing this process, something ever so slightly outside of our comfort zone, is persuasive.

Escaping Autopilot

At the height of this youthful ignorance I was the classic definition of a mindless stereotype, flying through days without really taking into consideration what I was doing. Many people go through their lives in this autopilot mode: gulping down food; rushing around in a wired attempt to be constantly 'doing'; not really listening to anyone who they come into contact with; present in body but not in mind. It leaves us beginning and ending days feeling fractured, a vicious cycle of exhaustion as we try to catch up with ourselves. Ultimately, it also makes us less productive, less joyful and more stressed.

In this situation it is difficult to be objective and look outside of ourselves. Andy Hargreaves and Michael Fullan (2012) highlight how teaching can 'rob us of the time to take stock, to be mindful of what we are really doing and why'. They urge their readers to 'be mindful. Begin with yourself'. Reflecting on the following questions from *Mindfulness* (2011) by Mark Williams and Danny Penman, is a useful starting point in this process. It will aid us in considering whether we are in falling into some of the autopilot traps:

1. Do you find it difficult to stay focused on what's happening in the present?

2. Do you tend to walk quickly to get to where you're going without paying attention to what you experience along the way?

3. Does it seem as if you are 'running on automatic', without much awareness of what you are doing?

4. Do you rush through activities without being really attentive to them?

5. Do you get so focused on the goal you want to achieve that you lose touch with what you are doing right now to get there?

6. Do you find yourself preoccupied with the future or the past?

The answers to these questions can identify barriers not only to a positive and happy life, but effective teaching in the classroom. It prevents any kind of immersion in our teaching, resulting in lessons in which we are never fully present to assist the students we teach or build positive relationships.

The Benefits of Meditation

The explosion in popularity of mindfulness and meditation is not without reason. Since realising that these practices do not require us to sit cross-legged, humming and surrounded be a sea of incense burners, I have found my relationship with stress and organisation have markedly improved through doing these activities. My ability to maintain concentration and listen more attentively has also developed, and I have a better understanding of my own behaviour. Daniel Goleman and Richard Davidson (2017) suggest that 'Meditation is an excellent way to enhance emotional intelligence skills, especially self-awareness'. It also has the added benefit of reducing anxiety and has been shown to have a very positive impact in the treatment of depression.

There are also clear health benefits with engaging in meditation. In *Change Your Thinking with CBT* (2012), Dr Sarah Edelman states that the physical results of meditation are:

A slowdown in the rate of our heartbeat

A slowdown in our breathing rate

A drop in blood pressure

A relaxation of muscle tension

A drop in oxygen consumption.

The Meditation Process

Meditation can be most aptly described as taking some time out of the endless pace, noise and expectations of the day to sit in silence, replenish our energy, and focus on our breathing. The long-term goal is to settle the mind – not into some kind of lethargic apathy, but into a state of calm alertness. While the simplicity of this sounds refreshingly appealing, there are challenges. The most irritating of these is that our wired minds fly instantly to the multiple thoughts that are lurking subconsciously.

The first attempt at meditating often feels the most unusual and ultimately unsuccessful, and is almost inevitably coupled with a 'what on earth am I doing?' feeling throughout. First, it is important to find somewhere quiet in which you will not be disturbed. Then, it is about sitting in a chair with a straight but comfortable back (the slow posture comes into force here!) and shoulders relaxed.

After this, it is remarkably simple: close your eyes and focus on your breathing. The temptation is to overcomplicate this, but this is the basic foundation of meditation. It might be helpful to begin to count your breaths; this will aid in focusing the mind. The purpose is not to control or exaggerate the breathing, but to allow it to flow naturally. Instead, you try to focus your attention on the breath moving, with each inhalation and exhalation.

When you inevitably start to become distracted (perhaps Ryan, that devilish Year 9 student, will pop into your mind and refuse to drift off!), it is important not to panic or become frustrated. You should return to the breath and begin counting again. Calmly re-focusing back on your breathing will soon help in dissipating any unwelcome thoughts. Even in a meditation that feels like more of a battle than Ryan's class, you will find that you emerge from it feeling a sense of clarity and calm that was missing before.

The next challenge is to move beyond isolated attempts at meditating when life is feeling particularly stressful by creating a routine. Starting small, with five- or ten-minute sessions will help; attempting epic seventy-minute meditations will only put you off. Using a timer on a phone or a watch will also prevent your mind wandering into uncertainty about when your meditating adventure will reach its conclusion.

There are some excellent websites that can support fledgling meditation attempts. Headspace.com is a particularly good one to provide an introduction to meditating. Books I have referenced in this chapter, such as *Mindfulness: a practical guide to finding peace in a frantic world* by Mark Williams and Danny Penman, provide a twelve-week programme that can structure and motivate the start of meditating. There will be struggles and frustrations, and you will question your sanity as you seek to temper the range of thoughts that come flooding in uninvited to this serenity. The important thing is to try to enjoy the peace and individual time that it will afford, and remember the value of the long-term goals. As Eckhart Tolle (2001) points out, 'the mind is a superb instrument when used rightly'. Our minds can be strengthened through this practice, and the patience, focus and concentration that meditation cultivates are positive for many different aspects of life.

The Disciplined Approach

I had a fairly sporadic relationship with meditation for the first year or so (don't worry; I will spare you those fascinating details!) For me it has worked most positively when there is an element of discipline; that is, when it is embedded in a daily routine. I now meditate first thing in the morning when I wake up, although the imminent arrival of my first child might just result in a slight change in this habit! The clarity and peace of mind that meditation can give you before the day begins is refreshing; it sets you up for a day in which control and direction will be palpable. There is also an element of positivity involved; instead of beginning the day in autopilot, it begins with a moment to collect our thinking and prepare mentally.

It might be that it works best for you at the end of the day, allowing a sense of closure. Nelson Mandela, a stoical meditator, wrote: 'regular meditation, say of about fifteen minutes a day before you turn in, can be fruitful in this regard' (Sampson, 2011).

Either way, embedding new routines and learning meditation is not easy. However, as Greg McKeown (2014) notes, perseverance will pay off:

> Once we master them [a new skill] and make them automatic we have won an enormous victory, because the skill remains with us for the rest of our lives. Once they are in place they are gifts that keep on giving.

In times of stress and challenge, meditation can be a steady activity we return to – energising us and helping us to find calm in our busy worlds. The famous Chinese proverb 'quiet thoughts mend the body' is particularly relevant for us as teachers.

Mindful Days

While there will be immediate positive aspects to developing a meditation habit of ten minutes a day, it will not provide any lasting solutions if we continue to race mindlessly through the rest of the day. Instead, actively trying to find moments of mindfulness throughout the day can sustain this feeling of objectivity and quiet. It will also prevent us from endlessly fretting about the future, allowing us to focus on the present and what we can immediately influence and control (the stoical philosophers are nodding sagely in agreement!)

In doing so, we embrace what Thich Nhat Hanh – who has been dubbed 'the world's calmest man' – calls 'the beginners mind'. As he states, 'mindfulness helps you go home to the present. And every time you go there and recognize a condition of happiness that you have, happiness comes' (Nhat Hanh, 1992). Some ways to achieve this during the day are:

1. **The mindful walk:** In his famous poem 'Leisure', William Henry Davies asks 'what is this life, if full of care/we have no time to stand and stare'. Taking time to be present and aware of our surroundings can help us to recognise all the positives that are around us. There is no better time to do this than on one of the walks we take every day. Instead of internalising and fixating on possible worries, we take the time to look carefully at what really surrounds us. Even better is to take a deliberate mindful walk, with the aim of looking at the world through a new lens. As Henry David Thoreau (1908) suggested 'you cannot perceive beauty but with a serene mind'.

2. **Mindful tea and coffee:** Back to our superbly serene monk, Thich Nhat Hanh (1992): 'Suppose you are drinking a cup of tea. When you hold your cup, you may like to breathe it in, to bring your mind back to your body, and you become fully present'. No matter how busy we are, we can give ourselves time each day to enjoy a simple hot drink. We will return to action after this break feeling even more energised than before.

3. **Mindful eating:** One of the first ways to discover how much of our days are spent going about on autopilot is to reflect on how we eat. Do we guzzle down our food, never stopping to taste or savour what we are effectively inhaling? The mindful eating approach involves being present when we eat: holding, seeing, and tasting the food. Our lunchtimes in school, despite the various things we could be doing, are primed for some slow, savoured and mindful lunch eating, or even just some mindful conversation!

Ten minutes to pause and break from our rushed existence is manageable, no matter how busy we are. By investing this time, we begin to build a better relationship with stress, and can then present a much calmer version of ourselves to the world. As Marcus Aurelius (2004) would have it, 'he who lives in harmony with himself lives in harmony with the universe'.

Slow Questions

1. How much of your day is spent on autopilot; present in body but not mind?

2. Could you put ten minutes aside for yourself a day?

3. What meditating routine would work best for you?

4. How else could you use mindfulness throughout the day?

5. Could you make time for some mindful eating or walking?

CHAPTER 21:
VALUE-DRIVEN LEADERSHIP

If your actions inspire others to dream more, learn more, do more and become more, you are a leader.
John Quincy Adams

Having taken tentative steps into leadership early in my own teaching career, this chapter comes with some recognition about the degree of challenge that moving into a leadership position in a school provides. What makes effective leadership is an endlessly complex subject; one that I would certainly not claim to be anything near an expert in. However, the experience of leadership, followed by a return to full-time teaching in the classroom, has led to much reflection on how it can be interpreted from both sides of the staffroom. This chapter will identify what I believe to be the core slow leadership values that may have the potential to drive improvements in schools and increase staff wellbeing.

There is a profound change of thinking that must take place in the transition from classroom teacher to a leadership role. With this transition comes a significant increase in responsibility, pressure and expectations of delivery. You are quickly expected to become not only a role model, but an embodiment of the values and ethos of the school.

The reality is that the slow values that have dominated this book are even more applicable to those at leadership level. While it is challenging, taking on a leadership position can also be hugely inspiring and rewarding. It vastly increases the impact that we can have on students and, as we shall discuss, the best leaders have this clarity of moral purpose at the core of all they do.

Why?

Simon Sinek (2011) has noted that being attuned to your purpose and motivation is an important basis for good leadership:

> Charisma has nothing to do with energy; it comes from a clarity of WHY. It comes from absolute conviction in an ideal bigger than oneself.

Energy, in contrast, comes from a good night's sleep or lots of caffeine. Energy can excite. But only charisma can inspire. Charisma commands loyalty. Energy does not.

To be effective, school leaders should possess motivation and drive that is inspired from an unshakable belief in the potential of young people to achieve. Those who enter leadership positions for egotistical benefits or financial reasons (not that there are many in teaching!) will not challenge, excite or inspire staff. In order to sustain themselves through the demands of leadership, school leaders need to know why they are investing so much of themselves in this demanding role. This conviction will motivate them when things inevitably become more challenging. As Will Ryan (2008) notes:

> Our greatest school leaders have four great personal traits or qualities. These are interconnected. The overriding quality is passion... Great school leaders have discovered a reason, a consuming, energising, almost obsessive purpose that drives them forward. It galvanises them to become bigger, bolder people and sustains them through difficult times.

It is not a question of natural temperament that will define how well a person leads. As such, it is no coincidence that the best teachers in the classroom often go on to make the best leaders, as many of the necessary qualities are mirrored. Some of the quietest people I have met have been excellent leaders, while some of the most extroverted have been the worst. Good leadership is about authenticity and a person's ability to radiate genuine commitment and integrity. To do this, it is important that there is a quiet, understated confidence surrounding the individual, one that speaks of knowledge of self and can inspire others.

While temperament and the quality of humility is vital, the remainder of this chapter will propose a set of leadership essentials – the important aspects that fuel successful leadership at any level.

Essential: Manager and a Leader

The influence that leaders exert in a school cannot be underestimated. The tone, direction and interpersonal focus of a school is profoundly influenced through their actions. They are constantly under the microscope of staff and students, where their behaviour signals what is acceptable and unacceptable on so many different levels. Their scope of influence means they have the potential to have a discernible impact on how we feel about our work.

There needs to be a clear distinction between a manger and a leader in a school capacity. Both are essential, but it is leadership that will ensure that people buy into a vision and feel a collaborative sense of purpose. Perhaps the easiest way to expand on this is by exploring what is at the heart of any successful school: relationships.

A manager will pragmatically seek to build systems and mechanisms to ensure that things function smoothly; a leader on the other hand will manage to build loyalty and trust through these systems. A leader will coach others and try to bring out the best in those around them; a manager will seek to assign tasks and tell people what to do. Leaders will generate followers who want to work for them, while managers will have people who do things for them.

The reality is that a manager is defined by speed and detachment, whereas a leader will model the slow values that permeate this book: listening, patience, attention, reflection, strategic direction, and investment in relationships. We need both to function well in any organisation, yet it is much more nurturing and inspiring to be led rather than to be managed.

Essential: Attention to Detail

One of the aspects that was drummed into me as a fledgling leader was the necessity to have complete and utter attention to detail. It is very simple: without the sense of care, commitment and time invested in presenting the best to staff and students, there will not be the same sense of care resonating throughout the school walls. It is about being a credible, committed professional in the eyes of those that are being guided by leaders. Without the necessary slowing down that this requires, we present ourselves as disorganised and rushed – generating more stress for those who we are trying to lead.

Essential: Long-Term Visions

There needs to be a core purpose running through a school that goes beyond platitudes or mission statements. These are the set of values that a school makes its decisions from, and these are values that leaders must refuse to compromise on. Mary Myatt (2016a) notes how this approach allows for transparency:

> There is simplicity and power in returning to our main goals. People working in schools where there is clarity report not only greater focus, but a sense of security in knowing that the major item in meetings is strongly linked to the major goal for overall school improvement, and that they are all clear about what their contribution needs to be.

These goals need to be a strategic road map which are patiently followed in order to achieve long-term success. Perhaps the most obvious overriding question for a school leader to reflect on is this: are we streamlining everything to make sure staff can do their jobs in a better and more efficient manner? With extra time afforded to making decisions and a less physically demanding daily routine, it is vital that staff in leadership positions do not lose the perspective of what life is like 'at the chalk face' on a full teaching timetable.

Frustrations are inevitably caused in schools when management forget to acknowledge this in their decision-making; such as when things are overcomplicated, or time is being wasted on things that are superfluous. Meetings are crucial in this endeavour. So often, time is lost in meetings, particularly when they appear to be taken up by 'business' that could be easily disseminated in paper form or an email. Making sure the purpose of a meeting is clear by sharing an agenda well in advance so that things move swiftly will help ensure time is used wisely.

Essentials: Being Present

One of the loudest of teachers' frustrations with school leadership teams is a lack of presence and visibility. It is the 'shadow' leadership approach: delivering instructions then drifting back into dusty offices to look at the spreadsheet impact. While there may be an immeasurable amount of paperwork and office-based tasks that need completed, being out and about during the school day is one of the most important slow skills a leader can demonstrate.

It is time that validates itself on so many different levels: it shows teachers that the leadership of the school is right there alongside them, not divorced from the reality of what is happening around the school building. This also helps to secure positive attitudes and behaviours from students, as they are very clear on the expectations of them.

Essentials: Growing Teachers

In terms of the leadership values that can motivate and inspire staff to perform better, focusing on the reality of what most of us invest our time doing and thinking about is a significant energiser for teaching staff. Teachers want to talk about learning, they want to grow as teachers and they want to work in conditions that can enable them to do this. John Tomsett (2015) states that this is the principle of the school he leads in York – 'Ultimately, truly great schools don't suddenly exist. You grow teachers first, who, in turn, grow a truly great school. A truly great school grows like an oak tree over years, not a mushroom overnight'.

The beating heart of truly outstanding schools is the recognition that teaching can always be improved and developed. In these schools a refusal to accept complacency in the classroom filters through meaningful CPD programmes. These programmes are not about random one-off presentations of the latest educational fads that are then forgotten within weeks; instead, they build progressively on teachers' skills and knowledge.

Outstanding schools also prioritise giving staff time for professional dialogue, trusting them to use this in ways which will help them improve their teaching. Coaching and mentoring is one way in which this can be employed in order to build on the strengths and skill sets of individual staff members. This progress is not achieved by berating teachers with the Ofsted stick, but rather through maintaining an environment that priorities meaningful reflection.

Essentials: Collaboration

Andy Hargreaves and Michael Fullan (2012) have described the merits of teachers joining forces – 'Talk together, plan together, work together – that's the simple key'. The reality is that this often needs to be facilitated and led by those in leadership positions.

Enabling staff to have structured time to be collegiate is vital. It brings together the expertise that is hidden in different corners of the schools. Leaders need to give departments opportunities to share and prevent the duplication of planning and resources that is so often the case in schools.

Essentials: Workload

Some schools blindly ignore the fact that it is both staff and students that need to be looked after. The best schools manage to achieve this troublesome balance that Ronald S. Barth (1990) has said 'Constantly takes note of the stress and anxiety level on the one hand and standards on the other, all the while searching for the optimal relationship of low anxiety and high standards'.

Schools need to be aware of staff *and* students wellbeing and stress at all levels. It requires leaders to be reflective about the pressure they are putting staff under, considering the processes in aspects of school life that can have a demonstrable impact on wellbeing.

Marking is one aspect of teacher workload that leaders have the potential to influence positively. There is no evidence to suggest that marking in different coloured pens or providing streams of written feedback has any benefits in helping students to learn. Instead it just forces teachers into the time-stealing swapping of pens while they mark. It is a sure way to demotivate staff and result in frustration. A better approach is to be sensible and practical about expectations of feedback provided by staff to students. Giving staff clear models about the standards required will prevent any lack of clarity. Creating an environment in which workbooks and marking is an open conversation will also help to share good practice and the best ways in which to approach feedback.

Another burdensome task is the writing of reports. Are written reports really necessary in the modern school environment? Have they ever been an effective way for teachers to use time? Many schools are now removing written comments and releasing data. While this may be somewhat impersonal, all good teachers should keep parents regularly updated on how their children are getting on. It removes the endless hours of writing, or indeed proofreading reports, that can take up valuable time that could be used more meaningfully.

Email is another element of teaching that often takes up huge amounts of time. There are days when the inbox is frequently shouting at us while we try to teach. Being hounded by incessant emails disrupts not only our teaching, but our capacity to be mindful and present teachers. School leaders need to provide clear guidance about what is acceptable to email and what needs to be discussed in conversation. What emails also do is remove the face-to-face dialogue that is vital for building successful relationships. It is incredibly challenging to communicate the nuances of dialogue in email; we have all experienced the consequences of a poorly worded or rushed email.

Essentials: Reading

The best leaders model that they are intrinsically bound up with learning and developing both themselves and others. They go out of their way to find out as much as they can about a topic and recognise that there is a continual improvement associated with growing their character. They do this while being aware of a greater concept of self: knowing that they cannot effectively lead others without an understanding of their own strengths and weaknesses.

Schools are defined by their relationships. These relationships are assisted at each stage by the efficiency and effectiveness of leaders at all levels. The capacity to pause, reflect and slow down must begin at the top. Once this has been achieved, the possibilities are endless. It is fundamentally about having a clear understanding of our purpose, ourselves and the people around us: value-driven leadership.

Slow Questions

1. Are you clear on your motivation for teaching and leading?

2. Are you a visible leader in school? How do you measure your impact?

3. What values are important to you?

4. How are you demonstrating those values?

5. What policy processes could be streamlined to help staff?

6. Is wellbeing a conversation your school is having?

7. What are you doing to continue learning and developing?

CONCLUSIONS

It does not matter how slowly you go, as long as you do not stop.
Confucius

If there is one recurring theme that has resonated throughout this book it is that, as teachers, we feel an overwhelming need to move quickly, to plan quickly, to teach quickly and to mark quickly. The multiple demands on us mean that we can lose the ability to pause and make the best decisions about how to use our time effectively. It also means that, in this frantic existence, we lose what I hope has resonated throughout this book: the joy and passion for a unique and wonderful profession.

What we have seen is that, as individual teachers at all levels, we do have the ability to wrestle back control and insist that we look seriously at how we can become more efficient. It is a journey that begins with how we use our environments to manifest clarity, then progresses to more complex evaluations of how to refine and streamline our planning, teaching and marking, and concludes with a consideration of how to slow down ourselves in order to manage stress and anxiety. We owe this refusal to accept mindless teaching and functioning, not only to ourselves and the students we teach, but to future generations of inspiring teachers who might be put off by the narrative of the negative in our profession.

We also have to prioritise our own wellbeing, and refuse to accept trite maxims that herald teachers as being slaves to students. Acknowledging that burnout is a problem in teaching is an important step in making proactive changes for the future. Nobody can function well in the workplace when it is dominated by stress and anxiety; people thrive and find meaning when our minds are calm and composed. This filters through to the students that we teach; a strategic and serene sense of direction will provide them with the best possible means of doing well. Taking proactive steps to organise ourselves appropriately, looking after our mental health and making time to reflect, will go some way in helping us to find both the positives and the meaning in our work for the duration of our long careers.

Making changes in our professional approach is challenging; it requires discipline and commitment. In *Better*, Atul Gawande (2008) notes that:

> Arriving at meaningful solutions is an inevitably slow and difficult process. Nonetheless, what I saw was: better is possible. It does not take genius. It takes diligence. It takes moral clarity. It takes ingenuity. And above all, it takes a willingness to try.

While we may not be able to conquer all the demands of teaching, we can certainly see what happens when we decide to deliberately slow down. Doing so might just re-energise, inspire and fuel our motivation for what we care deeply about: young people and their future.

ACKNOWLEDGEMENTS

I would like to thank all the brilliant teachers I have had the pleasure of working with and learning from. Thank you to all at Holland Park School, which was an amazing learning curve and inspired this book; particularly to my wonderful mentor Judith Clulow. Thank you to all the excellent staff at Cramlington Learning Village, particularly the brilliant English department for their encouragement and enthusiasm.

Thank you to my mum and dad for all their love and support; two inspiring teachers who showed me, in my dad's case as a student in his English class, what a rewarding and meaningful profession teaching could be. Thank you also to Fergus and Stephen for all the endless brotherly support in times of need!

Thank you to Alex Sharratt at John Catt Educational. I am very grateful for this opportunity and for your enthusiasm for the project in its rather vague beginnings and throughout the process. I am also hugely grateful to those who have invested a long time in reading drafts, and provided such constructive feedback. Thank you also to Milo MacDermot for designing the brilliant cover concept.

Having read a huge range of books and blogs for this project, thank you to all the excellent writers whose work I have been inspired by. Thank you to Mary Myatt for providing the generous foreword to the book.

I am particularly grateful to my wonderful wife Fiona, who has read every word painstakingly carefully. The book, much like its writer, is immeasurably better for your input. Your patience, love and understanding throughout the long nights being married to a laptop has been amazing. Here is to happy (and slow) future.

REFERENCES

'EliminatingUnnecessaryWorkloadaroundMarking'ReportoftheIndependentTeacher Workload Review Group. [Accessed 12 August 2017]. www.gov.uk/government/ publications/reducing-teacher-workload-marking-policy-review-group-report.

'The Big Question 2016' An opinion survey of teachers and leaders NASUWT (Accessed 20 September 2017) www.nasuwt.org.uk/uploads/assets/uploaded/ c316d25b-d8d7-4595-bbb0f9181d0427d1.pdf

Aesop (1994) *Aesop's Fables*. Wordsworth Children's Classic.

Allison, S. and Tharby, A. (2015) *Making Every Lesson Count: Six Principles to Support Great Teaching and Learning*. Carmarthen: Crown House Publishing.

Anderson, C. (2017) *TED Talks: The Official TED guide to public speaking*. Boston: Houghton Mifflin Harcourt.

Aurelius, M. (2004) *Meditations*. W&N.

Bambrick-Santoyo, P. (2012) *Leverage Leadership: A Practical Guide to Building Exceptional Schools*. San Francisco, CA: Jossey-Bass.

Barth, R.S. (1990) *Improving Schools from Within: Teachers, Parents and Principals Can Make the Difference (Jossey Bass Education Series)*. San Francisco, CA: Jossey-Bass.

Barton, G. (2012) *Don't Call it Literacy!: What every teacher needs to know about speaking, listening, reading and writing*. Abingdon: Routledge.

Beck, I. L., McKeown, M. G. and Kucan, L. (2013) *Bringing Words to Life: Robust Vocabulary Instruction*. 2nd ed. New York: Guilford Press.

Berger, R. (2003) *An Ethic of Excellence: Building a Culture of Craftsmanship with Students*. Portsmouth, NH: Heinemann.

Birbalsingh, K. (2016) *Battle Hymn of the Tiger Teachers: The Michaela Way*. Woodbridge: John Catt Educational.

Bjork, R.A (1994). Memory and metamemory considerations in the training of human beings. In J. Metcalfe and A. Shimamura (Eds)., *Metcognition: Knowing about Knowing* (pp.185-205). Cambridge, MA: MIT Press.

Bjork, E. L. and Bjork, R. A. (2011) Making things hard on yourself, but in a good way: Creating desirable difficulties to enhance learning. In: M.A Gernsbacher, R.W. Pew, L.M. Hough and J.R Powerantz, eds. *Psychology and the real world: Essays illustrating fundamental contributions to society.* New York: Worth Publishers. pp. 55-64.

Borg, J. (2004) *Persuasion: The Art of Influencing People.* Upper Saddle River, NJ: Prentice Hall.

Brown, G. A. and Wragg, E. C. (2001) *Questioning in The Secondary School.* Abingdon: Routledge.

Brown, P. C., Roediger, H. L. and McDaniel, M. A. (2014) *Make it Stick: The Science of Successful Learning.* Cambridge, MA: Harvard University Press.

Buck, A. (2017) *Leadership Matters: How Leaders at All Levels Can Create Great Schools.* Woodbridge: John Catt Educational.

Cain, S. (2013) *Quiet: The Power of Introverts in a World That Can't Stop Talking.* London: Penguin Books.

Cannon. W (1915) *Bodily Changes in Pain, Hunger, Fear and Rage: An Account of Recent Researches into the Function of Emotional Excitement.* Appleton-Century-Crofts.

Carless, D. (2006) Differing perceptions in the feedback process. *Studies in Higher Education*, 31(2), pp. 219-33.

Carney (2016) My Position on Power Poses: http://faculty.haas.berkeley.edu/dana_carney/pdf_My%20position%20on%20power%20poses.pdf. Accessed 07.07.17

Chase, C. C., Chin, D. B., Oppezzo, M. A., & Schwartz, D. L. (2009). Teachable agents and the protégé effect: Increasing the effort towards learning. *Journal of Science Education and Technology*, 18(4), 334–352.

Christodoulou, D. (2017) *Making Good Progress: The Future of Assessment for Learning.* Oxford: Oxford University Press.

Cirillo, F. (2009) *The Pomodoro Teachnique,* Lulu.com

Clark, R.E., Kirschner P.A., Swiller, J. (2012) Putting Students on the Path to Learning: The Case for Fully Guided Instruction. *American Educator*, 36(1) Spring 2012. pp. 6-11.

Coe, R., Aloisi, C., Higgins, S. and Elliot Major, L. (2014) *What makes great teaching? Review of the underpinning research.* London: The Sutton Trust.

Coultas, V. (2007) *Constructive Talk in Challenging Classrooms: Strategies for Behaviour Management and Talk-based Tasks*. Abingdon: Routledge.

Crabbe, T. (2015) *Busy: How to thrive in a world of too much*. London: Piatkus.

Crenshaw, D. (2008) *The Myth of Multitasking: How "Doing it All" Gets Nothing Done*. San Francisco, CA: Jossey-Bass.

Cuddy, A. (2015, December) Your body language may shape who you are [Video file]. Retrieved from www.ted.com/talks/amy_cuddy_your_body_language_shapes_who_you_are

Cuddy, A. (2016) *Presence: Bringing Your Boldest Self to Your Biggest Challenges*. London: Orion.

Curtis, C. (2017) 'A Year of Writing Creatively, independently and silently' [Accessed 6 June 2017]. www.learningfrommymistakes.blogspot.co.uk

Davenport, B. (2016) *Declutter Your Mind: How to Stop Worrying, Relieve Anxiety, and Eliminate Negative Thinking*. CreateSpace Independent Publishing Platform.

Davenport, B. and Scott, S. J. (2015) *The 10-Minute Declutter: The Stress-Free Habit for Simplifying Your Home*. CreateSpace Independent Publishing Platform.

De Bono, E. (1999) *Simplicity*. London: Penguin Books.

De Botton, A. (2001) *The Consolations of Philosophy*. London: Penguin Books.

Deans for Impact (2016). Practice with Purpose: The Emerging Science of Teacher Expertise. Austin, TX: Deans for Impact. Accessed 08/09/17: www.deansforimpact.org/resourcse/practice-with-purpose.

Dickens, C. (1995) *Hard Times*. Essex: Longman.

Dix, P. (2017) *When the Adults Change, Everything Changes: Seismic Shifts in School Behaviour*. Carmarthen: Independent Thinking Press.

Drucker, P. (2008) *Managing Oneself*. Boston, MA: Harvard Business School Publishing Corporation.

Dweck, C. (2007) *Mindset: The new psychology of success*. New York: Ballantine Books.

Dweck, C. (2012) *Mindset: How you can fulfil your potential*. Robinson, Constable & Robinson LTD.

Dweck, C. (2016) How Praise Became a Consolation Prize. The Atlantic, [online] 16 December. Available at: www.theatlantic.com/education/archive/2016/12/how-praise-became-a-consolation-prize/510845/ [Accessed 10/07/17]

Edelman, S. (2012) *Change Your Thinking with CBT: Overcome stress, combat anxiety and improve your life.* London: Vermilion.

Education Endowment Foundation, Metacognition and Self-Regulation [Accessed 22 November 2017]. www.educationendowmentfoundation.org.uk/evidence-summaries/teacher-learning-toolkit

Engelmann, S. and Carnine, D. (1982)*Theory of instruction: Principles and applications.* New York: Irvington Publishers.

Epictetus (2008) *Discourses and Selected Writings.* London: Penguin Classics

Eyre, C. (2016) *The Elephant in the Staffroom: How to reduce stress and improve teacher wellbeing.* Abingdon: Routledge.

Fisher, AV, Goodwin, KE, Seltman, H (2014): 'Visual Environment, Attention Allocation, and Learning in Young Children: When Too Much of a Good Thing May Be Bad, *Psychological science,* 2014 – Sage Publications

Fletcher-Wood, H. (2016) *Ticked off: Checklists for Teachers, Students, School Leaders.* Carmarthen: Crown House Publishing.

Gawande, A. (2008) *Better: A Surgeon's Notes on Performance.* London: Profile Books.

Gilbert, I. (2012) *Essential Motivation in the Classroom.* Abingdon: Routledge.

Ginott, H.G. (1972) *Teacher and child: A Book for Parents and Teachers.* London: Macmillan.

Gladwell, M. (2007) *Blink: The Power of Thinking Without Thinking.* Little, Brown and Company

Goleman, D. and Davidson, R. (2017) *The Science of Meditation: How to Change your Brain, Mind and Body.* London: Penguin Life.

Goleman, D., Boyatzis, R.E. and McKee, A. (2003) *The New Leaders: Transforming the Art of Leadership* London: Time Warner Paperbacks.

Goleman, D.(1996) *Emotional Intelligence: Why it Can Matter More Than IQ.* London: Bloomsbury Publishing.

Goman, C. K. (2011) *The Silent Language of Leaders: How Body Language Can Help – or Hurt – How You Lead.* San Francisco, CA: Jossey-Bass.

Hanushek, E. A. and Rivkin, S. G. (2006) Teacher Quality. *Handbook of the Economics of Education*, Volume 2, Amsterdam.

Hargreaves, A. and Fullan, M. (2012) Professional Capital: Transforming Teaching in Every School. *Teachers College Press*, 34(3) (June 2013)

Hattie, J. (2012) *Visible Learning for Teachers.* Abingdon: Routledge.

Hattie, J. and Timperley, H. (2007) The power of feedback. *Review of Educational Research*, 77 (1), pp. 81–112.

Hattie, J. and Yates, G. C. R. (2013) *Visible Learning and the Science of How we Learn.* Abingdon: Routledge.

Heath, C. and Heath, D. (2007) *Made to Stick: Why Some Ideas Take Hold and Others Come Unstuck.* London: Random House Business Books .

Heath, C. and Heath, D. (2011) *Switch: How to change things when change is hard.* London: Random House Business Books.

Hendrick, C. and Macpherson, R. (2017) *What Does This Look Like In The Classroom?: Bridging The Gap Between Research And Practice.* Woodbridge: John Catt Educational.

Henley, W. E, (2015) 'Poems' White Press

Hirsch, E. D. (2013) The key to increasing upward mobility is expanding vocabulary. *A Wealth Of Words, Education: The Social Order,* Winter 2013.

Hirsch, E. D. (1996) *The Schools We Need: And Why We Don't Have Them.* New York: Doubleday.

Honore, C. (2005) *In Praise of Slow: How a Worldwide Movement is Challenging the Cult of Speed.* London: Orion Books.

James, W. (2017) *The Principles of Psychology, Vols. 1-2.* Combined ed. CreateSpace Independent Publishing Platform.

Kahneman, D. (2012) *Thinking, Fast and Slow.* London: Penguin Books.

Kakutani, M. (2017) Obama's Secret to Surviving the White House Years: Books. *The New York Times* [online], 16 January. Available at: www.nytimes.com/20017/01/16/books/obamas-secret-to-surviving-the-white-house-years-books.html [Accessed 8 October 2017].

Leaming, B. (2010) *Churchill Defiant: Fighting on 1945–1955.* London: Harper Press.

Lemov, D. (2010) *Teach Like a Champion: 49 Techniques that Put Students on the Path to College*. San Francisco, CA: Jossey-Bass.

Lemov, D. (2015) *Teach Like a Champion 2.0: 62 Techniques that Put Students on the Path to College*. San Francisco, CA: Jossey-Bass.

Levitin, D. J. (2015) *The Organized Mind: Thinking Straight in the Age of Information Overload*. London: Penguin Books.

Lightfoot, L. (2016) Nearly half of England's teachers plan to leave in next five years. *The Guardian*, [online] 22 March. Available at: www.theguardian.com/education/2016/mar/22/teachers-plan-leave-five-years-survey-workload-england [Accessed 12 September 2017].

Mahrabian, A. (1981) *Silent Messages: Implicit Communication of Emotions and Attitude*. 2nd revised ed. Belmont, CA: Wadsworth Publishing Company.

Marland, M. (1993) *The Craft of the Classroom: A Survival Guide to Classroom Management in the Secondary School*. Portsmouth, NH: Heinemann Educational.

Mccrea, P. (2015) *Lean Lesson Planning: A practical approach to doing less and achieving more in the classroom*. CreateSpace Independent Publishing Platform.

Mccrea, P. (2017) *Memorable Teaching: Leveraging memory to build deep and durable learning in the classroom*. CreateSpace Independent Publishing Platform.

McGonigal, K. (2015) *The Upside of Stress: Why stress is good for you (and how to get good at it)*. London: Vermilion

Medina, J. (2014) *Brain Rules: 12 Principles for Surviving and Thriving at Work, Home, and School*. Seattle, WA: Pear Press.

Millburn, J. F. and Nicodemus, R. (2012) *Minimalism Essential Essays*. Missoula, MT: Asymmetrical Press.

Myatt, M. (2016a) *High Challenge, Low Threat: How the Best Leaders Find the Balance*. Woodbridge: John Catt Educational.

Myatt, M. (2016b) *Hopeful Schools* Woodbridge: Mary Myatt Learning Limited;

Newmark, B. (2017) What is Good Direct Instruction? Bennewmark.wordpress.com [blog] April 13th 2017 www.bennewmark.wordpess.com/2017/04/13/direct-instruction. [Accessed 20 November 2017].

Nhat Hanh, T. (1992) *Being Peace: Classic teachings from the world's most revered meditation master*. Berkeley, CA: Parallax Press.

Nuthall, G. (2007) *The Hidden Lives of Learners*. Wellington: NZCER Press.

Paul, R.W. and Elder, L. (2000) *Role of Questions in Teaching, Thinking and Learning. Critical Thinking: Basic Theory and Instructional Structures Handbook*. Foundation for Critical Thinking, 2000. Accessed from www.criticalthinking.org/pages/the-role-of-questions-in-teaching-thinking-and-learning/524.

Pinker, S. (2015) *The Language Instinct: How the Mind Creates Language*. New York: Harper Perennial.

Quigley, A. (2016) *The Confident Teacher: Developing successful habits of mind, body and pedagogy*. London: Routledge.

Ramlakhan, N. (2016) *Fast Asleep, Wide Awake: Discover the secrets of restorative sleep and vibrant energy*. London: Thorsons.

Rigney, D. (2010) *The Matthew Effect: How Advantage Begets Further Advantage*. New York: Columbia University Press.

Robinson, M. (2013) *Trivium 21C: Preparing young people for the future with lessons from the past*. Carmarthen: Independent Thinking Press

Rodenburg P. (2015) *The Right to Speak*. London: Bloomsbury Muthuen Drama.

Roediger, H. L., Putnam, A. L. and Smith, M. A. (2011) Ten benefits of testing and their applications to educational practice. In: J. Mestre and B. Ross (Eds.), *Psychology of Learning and Motivation: Cognition in Education* (pp 1-36) Oxford: Elsevier.

Rogers, B. (2007) *Behaviour Management: A Whole-school Approach*. London: Paul Chapman Publishing.

Rosenshine, B. (2012) Principles of Instruction: Research based principles that all teachers should know. *American Educator*, Spring 2012. Available at: www.aft.org/pdfs/americaneducator/spring2012/Rosenshine.pdf [Accessed 12.09.17]

Rowe, M. B. (1987) Wait time: Slowing down may be a way of speeding up. *American Educator* 11 (Spring 1987); pp. 38-43.

Russell, B. (2013) *The Conquest of Happiness*. Liveright Publishing Corporation.

Ryan, W. (2008) *Leadership with a Moral Purpose: Turning Your School Inside Out*. Carmarthen: Crown House Publishing.

Sadler, D. R. (1989). Formative assessment and the design of instructional systems. *Instructional Science*, 18(2), 119-144.

Sampson, A. (2011) *Mandela: The Authorised Biography.* UK ed. London: HarperPress.

Sampson, G. (1922) *English for the English: A Chapter on National Education.* Cambridge: Cambridge University Press.

Seneca, L. (2003) *Letters From A Stoic And Three Dialogues.* Translated from Latin by Robin Campbell. London: The Folio Society.

Sherrington, T. (2017) *The Learning Rainforest: Great Teaching in Real Classrooms.* Woodbridge: John Catt Educational Ltd.

Shulman, L. S. (2004) *The Wisdom of Practice – Collected Essays of Lee Shulman: Vol. 1.* San Francisco: Jossey-Bass.

Sinek, S. (2011) *Start with Why: How Great Leaders Inspire Everyone to Take Action.* London: Portfolio Penguin.

National Audit Office (2008) *Skills for Life: Progress in Improving Adult Literacy and Numeracy.* [web] 6 June 2008. Available at: www.nao.org.uk/wp-content/uploads/2008/06/0708482.pdf [Accessed 12 August 17]

Sleepio, Great British Sleep Survey (2012) Available at: <www.greatbritishsleepsurvey.com> [Accessed 8 September 2017].

Soderstrom, N. C. and Bjork, R. A. (2015) Learning Versus Performance. In: D.S. Dunn, ed. *Oxford Bibliographies Online: Psychology.* New York: Oxford University Press.

Stipek, D. (2010) How Do Teachers' Expectations Affect Student Learning? www.education.com/reference/article/teachers-expectations-affect-learning/

Sunim, H. (2017) *The Things You Can See Only When You Slow Down.* Translated from Korean by Chi-Young Kim. London: Penguin Books.

Sutton, R., Hornsey, M.J., & Douglas, K.M. (Eds., 2011) *Feedback: The communication of praise, criticism, and advice.* Peter Lang Publishing: New York.

Sweller, J. (1988) Cognitive Load During Problem Solving: Effects on Learning. *Cognitive Science*, Lawrence Erlbaum Associates, Inc.

Tapscott, D. (2009) *Grown up Digital: How the Net Generation is Changing Your World.* New York: McGraw-Hill Education.

Thaler, R. H. and Sunstein, C. R. (2010) *Nudge: Improving Decisions about Health, Wealth, and Happiness.* Concordville, PA.: Soundview Executive Book Summaries.

Tharby, A. (2017) *Making Every English Lesson Count: Six principles to support great reading and writing*. Carmarthen: Crown House Publishing.

Theobald, J., (2017) Teaching: If You Aren't Dead Yet, You Aren't Doing it Well Enough. [blog] Available at: www.othmarstrombone.wordpress.com [Accessed 10 October 17].

Thoreau, H. D. (1908) *Walden, or, Life in the woods*. London: J.M. Dent.

Tolle, E. (2001) *The Power of Now: A Guide to Spiritual Enlightenment*. London: Yellow Kite.

Tomsett, J. (2015) *This Much I Know about Love Over Fear: Creating a culture of truly great teaching*. Carmarthen: Crown House Publishing.

Turner, S. (2016) *Secondary Assessment and Curriculum*. London: Bloomsbury Education.

Wasmund, S. and Wakefield, H. (2016) *Do Less, Get More*. London: Penguin Life.

Wiliam, D. (2014) Redesigning Schooling – 8 Principled Curriculum Design SSAT The Schools Network. [online] Available at: webcontent.ssatuk.co.uk/wp-content/uploads/2013/09/RS8-Principled-assessment-design-chapter-one.pdf [Accessed 8 August 2017]

Wiliam, D. (2016) The 9 things every teacher should know. [web] 2 September 2016. Available at: <www.tes.com/us/new/breaking-views/9-things-every-teacher-should-know> [Accessed 19 November 2017].

Williams, M. and Penman, D. (2011) *Mindfulness: A practical guide to finding peace in a frantic world*. London: Piatkus.

Willingham D. T, (2010) *Why Don't Students Like School?: A Cognitive Scientist Answers Questions About How the Mind Works and What It Means for the Classroom*. London: Jossey Bass.

Willingham, D. T. (2007) Critical Thinking: Why is it so hard to teach. *American Educator*, 31, 8-19.

Willingham, D. T. (2009) What Will Improve a Student's Memory. *American Educator*. Available at: www.aft.org/sites/default/files/periodicals/willingham_0.pdf

Willingham, D. T. (2017) *The Reading Mind: A Cognitive Approach to Understanding How the Mind Reads* San Francisco: Jossey-Bass

Willingham, D. T. (2008) How Praise can motivate – or stifle. *American Educator*, 29 (4), 23-27, 48.

Winne, P. H. and Marx, R. W. (1983) *Students' cognitive processes while learning from teaching.* (Final Report Volume 1). Bunaby, BC: Simon Fraser University, Faculty of Education.

Wiseman, R. (2015)*Night School: The Life-Changing Science of Sleep.* Unabridged ed. London: Pan.

Van Gogh, V. (1997) *The Letters of Vincent Van Gogh.* New Ed Edition London: Penguin Classics.